C000127652

The
Connell Guide
to
Charles Dickens's

Great Expectations

by
John Sutherland & Jolyon Connell

Contents

Introduction   4

A summary of the plot   6

What is *Great Expectations* about?   10

What makes the opening scenes so
powerful?   20

Is Pip a snob?   29

Why does Pip feel so drawn to Satis
House?   42

How real is Pip's love for Estella?   48

What is the significance of Magwitch?   58

How corrupt is the world Dickens shows
us in *Great Expectations*?   74

Is Orlick Pip's "double"?   83

Is *Great Expectations* a misogynist novel?   90

How plausible is the ending of the novel?   103

What view of life does *Great Expectations*
leave us with?   107

NOTES

Bildungsroman   *12*

Dickens's use of humour   *16*

Education   *22*

The marshes   *26*

Dickens and class   *32*

The original Miss Havisham   *44*

Sex in Great Expectations   *50*

The Criminal Code   *59*

Ten facts about Great Expectations   *64*

Dickens at work, by his eldest son, Charley   *68*

Pip's reliability as a narrator   *78*

Biddy   *90*

The importance of hands   *98*

Pip's journey down the Thames   *100*

Modern critics   *114*

A short chronology   *120*

Bibliography   *122*

Introduction

Few works of English literature have been more loved than *Great Expectations*. Originally published, in serial form, in the weekly newspaper, *All the Year Round*, which Charles Dickens owned and ran, it has always been one of the best-selling Victorian novels of our time. No Dickens work, with the exception of *A Christmas Carol*, has been adapted more for both film and television.

It has been as popular with critics as it has with the public. Early reviews were mixed, with the influential *Blackwoods* magazine finding it "feeble, fatigued, colourless", and the American *Atlantic Monthly* lamenting that "some of the old hilarity and play of fancy has gone..." But later critics have been more or less unanimous in their praise. In 1937 George Bernard Shaw called the novel Dickens's "most compactly perfect book". John Lucas describes it as "the most perfect and the most beautiful of all Dickens's novels", Angus Wilson as "the most completely unified work of art that Dickens ever produced".

Great Expectations has been so successful partly because it's an exciting story. Dickens always had a keen eye on the market and subscribed to Wilkie Collins's advice: "make 'em laugh, make 'em cry, above all make 'em wait." From the violent opening scene on the marshes to the climax of Magwitch's attempted escape on the

Thames, the story is full of suspense, mystery and drama. But while these elements of *Great Expectations* have ensured its popularity, it is also a novel which, as this guide will seek to show, raises profound questions not just about the nature of Victorian society but about the way human relationships work and the extent to which people are shaped by their childhoods and the circumstances in which they grow up.

Henry Hull as Magwitch in the 1934 American film adaptation

A summary of the plot

The hero of *Great Expectations*, "Pip" (christened Philip Pirrip), is an orphan, brought up by his much older sister and her husband, Joe Gargery. Joe is a good-hearted blacksmith who treats Pip kindly. Mrs Joe is a cane-wielding tyrant. Visiting his family's graves on Christmas Eve, in a deserted graveyard in the marshes, Pip is jumped on by a convict on the run from the "hulks" – prison-ships lying in the mouth of the nearby Medway estuary. Terrified, he agrees to steal food for the convict, as well as a file to saw off his manacles. Later, when the convict, Abel Magwitch, is recaptured, he does not betray Pip. Nor does he forget Pip's kindness.

Pip's apprenticeship in Joe's forge, a year or two later, is preceded by a strange summons to visit the imperious Miss Havisham in nearby Satis House. Abandoned at the altar 20 years earlier she has kept its interior, and her dress, and even the wedding table feast (now rotted and food for mice) exactly as it was on the day, when she was jilted.

At her ruined and shuttered house, Pip is humiliated and tormented by Miss Havisham's young ward, Estella. He nonetheless falls hopelessly in love with Estella.

After several visits to Satis House, Pip is called on by an inscrutable London lawyer, Jaggers, who informs him that he now has "expectations" – a handsome bequest is in prospect. He, Jaggers, is not free to say who the mysterious benefactor is. Pip naturally assumes it to be Miss Havisham, the heiress to a great brewing fortune.

Now Pip can rise in life. He goes off to London to pursue the goal of becoming a "gentleman". Joe and the housekeeper, Biddy, whom he leaves behind, are heartbroken. In London, which he has never visited before, he lodges in the city's legal quarter, with Herbert Pocket – a young clerk, distantly related to Miss Havisham. Herbert has no expectations whatsoever and slaves in an insurance office. He and Pip become friends. Pip also befriends Wemmick, Jaggers's head clerk, one of the more amiable characters in the novel.

Now a man about town, Pip still aspires to marry Estella, who has become a serial breaker of men's hearts, as Miss Havisham has trained her to be. She is cold as ice towards Pip, out of kindness as she perversely tells him, because she actually cares for him, and would rather not break *his* heart. But she will never love him, or any man. She cannot.

Pip learns that his sister has been savagely attacked and left a helpless invalid. Dolge Orlick, a journeyman blacksmith dismissed by Joe, is suspected. One night, when alone – aged 23, and about to come into his fortune – Pip is visited by Abel Magwitch, the escaped convict he helped on

the marshes. To his dismay, Magwitch, alias
Provis, turns out to be his benefactor. Having
prospered as a sheep-farmer in Australia he
decided to use his money to create a gentleman "of
my own", both in gratitude to Pip and as an act of
revenge against his accomplice, Compeyson, who,
because he was a gentleman, was treated leniently
by the court for the same offence (forgery) as led
to his being transported for life. Having come back
without leave, Magwitch will be hanged if caught.
Pip, mortified as he is, gives his patron refuge but
refuses to accept any more of his money.

He visits Miss Havisham to protest at her
having cruelly misled him and learns that
Estella is to marry oafish Bentley Drummle,
a "gentleman" by birth with aristocratic
connections. Estella has no feeling for Drummle
or any man. She is simply carrying through Miss
Havisham's merciless campaign against the
male sex.

On a subsequent visit, in which Miss Havisham
finally implores Pip's forgiveness, the old woman
dies as the result of a fire which burns Satis House
to the ground. Pip himself is badly injured trying
to save her. It emerges that Magwitch is Estella's
father. (Her mother, Molly, is Jaggers's housekeeper.) Magwitch's mortal foe, Compeyson, is,
it further transpires, the man who jilted Miss
Havisham at the altar. Dickens was never a
novelist frightened by coincidence or improbability.

After nearly being murdered in an encounter on the marshes with his old enemy, Orlick, Pip tries to help Magwitch escape. His efforts are foiled by Compeyson, who – still making mischief – has found out what is going on and has tipped off the police. In a desperate fight in the waters of the Thames, Compeyson is drowned and Magwitch mortally wounded. He dies in the condemned cell of Newgate prison. Pip, having contracted jail-fever as a result of his visits to the jail, is nursed back to health by Joe, who nobly pays off Pip's debts – Magwitch's fortune being confiscated by the crown – thus stopping him being sent to the debtors' prison. Pip then returns home to ask Biddy to marry him but finds she is already married – to Joe.

Penniless, he becomes a clerk, and goes off to work abroad alongside Herbert. Eleven years later he returns to visit Joe and Biddy. In the ruins of Satis House he is reunited with Estella whom he finds walking there. (Estella's husband, Drummle, has been killed by a horse he was abusing.) The narrative suggests that they may at last marry but the ending is left deliberately ambiguous.

What is *Great Expectations* about?

At the heart of *Great Expectations* – as searching an exploration of Victorian civilisation and its values as can be found in literature – lies this exchange between Pip and Biddy, the housekeeper at the forge.

> *"Biddy," said I, after binding her to secrecy,*
> *"I want to be a gentleman."*
> *"Oh, I wouldn't, if I was you!" she returned.*
> *"I don't think it would answer." (17)**

The idea of becoming a gentleman is almost synonymous with the Victorian era. A variety of factors, from the rapid pace of industrialisation and urbanisation to the invention of the railways, better schools and a greater emphasis on the professions, combined to make raising oneself up – moving into a higher sphere of life – seem much more possible than it had in the more settled rural England of the 18th century. It was a time when one could have "great expectations", or at least greater expectations than one's parents had had.

Dickens's great rival, Thackeray, was as preoccupied as Dickens was with the idea of

*Throughout this book, the numbers in brackets refer to the chapters from which quotations are taken.

gentility and his own fiction, notably *Vanity Fair*, as his biographer, Gordon Ray, suggests, calls for a "redefinition" of gentlemanliness for an age with a more fluid class structure. The Thackerayan redefinition involved detaching "nobility" as an exclusive property of the traditionally "noble" classes and relocating it in the middle classes who, Thackeray implies, were morally superior and in any case already rising to the top of English society in steadily greater numbers. The nobles in *Vanity Fair* – Sir Pitt Crawley, the Marquis of Steyne, etc. – are, all of them, utterly ignoble. It is Dobbin, the greengrocer's son, who is the true gentleman.

Dickens's own view of gentility is more complex, understandably so given his background. Thackeray, in a sense, wrote about gentlemen from "the inside". Born into a respectable family, and very much at home in the world of London clubs, his province, in W.C. Roscoe's words, is that "debateable land between the aristocracy and the middle classes". (Most of his main characters, even Dobbin, went to public school.) Dickens, on the other hand, had more slender claims to gentility: his grandfather had been a steward to Lord Crewe, his father a clerk in the Navy Pay Office who lost any claim to respectability when, after moving to London in 1822, he was imprisoned for debt. Dickens himself, in the most scarring experience of his life, was sent to work in a blacking factory, making all the more remarkable his subsequent transformation into successful author and self-made gentleman who eventually assumed the right to use the crest of the old Dickens family of Staffordshire.

His rapid rise led some contemporaries to question his ability to describe gentlemen, with a *Times* reviewer, writing about John Forster's biography of Dickens in 1871, observing unkindly that the author was "often vulgar in manners and dress... ill at ease in his intercourse with gentlemen..." The novelist and critic, G.K. Chesterton, offered a more enlightened perspective:

> When people say that Dickens could not describe a gentleman, what they mean is... that Dickens could not describe a gentleman as gentlemen feel

BILDUNGSROMAN

Great Expectations is often categorised under this German term. It applies to novels dealing with the youth and moral growth of a hero(ine), usually identifiable with the novelist writing the story. The term means, literally, "portrait novel" – for which read 'self-portrait'. In England, the Bildungsroman was in vogue during the 1840s and 1850s. Notable examples are Thackeray's *Pendennis*, Dickens's *David Copperfield*, George Eliot's *The Mill on the Floss* and, of course, *Great Expectations*.◆

a gentleman. They mean that he could not take that atmosphere easily, accept it as the normal atmosphere, or describe that world from the inside... Dickens did not describe gentlemen in the way that gentlemen describe gentlemen... He described them... from the outside, as he described any other oddity or special trade.

Although, like Thackeray, a novelist of middle-class emergence, Dickens was at the opposite end of the scale. As Robin Gilmour puts it in his masterly study, *The Idea of the Gentleman in the Victorian Novel*, he "is concerned with the lower reaches of the middle class in its most anxious phase of self-definition, struggling out of trade and domestic service and clerical work into the sunshine of respectability". But, in seeing gentlemen "from the outside", Dickens was (or had become, by the time of *Great Expectations*) much more sceptical about the concept of gentility and the way in which, however desirable it might be made to sound, it depended on the idea of *exclusion* – of separating the gentleman from the non-gentleman. His central preoccupation in *Great Expectations* is the relationship between respectable society and the underworld, between gentility and crime, between those lucky enough to have made it to the top and those left at the bottom, many of whom, often through no fault of their own, are forced into crime.

It has been suggested that Dickens's view in *Great Expectations* stemmed in part from the circumstances of his own life: the novelist famous for celebrating the values of hearth and home had broken, after 22 years of marriage, from his wife and taken up with a young actress, Ellen Ternan, thus becoming an outsider again.

Certainly his thinking on the nature of gentility and the extent to which it can be acquired, as opposed to inherited, had evolved in the years since he wrote his first orphan's story, *Oliver Twist*. As Gilmour points out, there are two conflicting impulses at the heart of this earlier novel: "a horror of the criminal underworld when seen through the terrified eyes of the child Oliver, and a sympathetic understanding of the same underworld from a different, more realistic and socially compassionate perspective". Dickens, who never forgot his experience in the blacking factory, understands why characters like Nancy, Bill Sikes and the Artful Dodger are as they are: he shows all too clearly why they have become criminals and equally clearly how Oliver finds in Fagin's den companionship and warmth, not to mention food, shelter and laughter, all of which had been denied him in the workhouse so-called respectable society provided for penniless orphans like Oliver, "despised by all, and pitied by none". (Fagin was even named after Bob Fagin, a boy who was kind

Opposite: poster for Alfonso Cuarón's 1998 film adaptation, starring Gwyneth Paltrow, Ethan Hawke, Robert De Niro and Anne Bancroft

to Dickens in the blacking factory.)

And yet, as Gilmour says, in *Oliver Twist* Dickens doesn't follow through on the idea that it is an accident of birth which condemns a child to the workhouse "and the fault of society that the road from the workhouse should lead so naturally to the life of crime". Quite the opposite. Oliver is rescued by fairy godparents, the Maylies and Mr Brownlow, and miraculously it turns out that he himself, after all, is the son of a gentleman. The novel may recognise the common humanity of Oliver and the Artful Dodger, but while one is reclothed and sent off to a smart school the other is transported. The underworld and

DICKENS'S USE OF HUMOUR

"I have made the opening, I hope, in its general effect exceedingly droll," wrote Dickens to his future biographer, John Forster, in October 1860. "I have put a child and a good-natured foolish man, in relations that seem to me very funny." It is often forgotten that *Great Expectations*, despite the painfulness of much of its material, is often very funny. Humour plays an important part in engaging our sympathies for Pip, as in the passage when Herbert educates him in table manners:

"Let me introduce the topic, Handel, by mentioning that in London it is not the custom to put the knife in the mouth – for fear of accidents – and that while the fork is

respectable society, the novel leaves us feeling, are utterly incompatible.

Dickens's second famous treatment of the orphan is similarly ambiguous. David Copperfield is a gentleman's son who nearly loses his birthright after his mother's death when he is set to work in a warehouse and then runs away, but in the end, like Oliver, he is symbolically reclothed and sent off to school. In David's case, the underworld he is plunged into is merely disreputable rather than criminal, but the novel has a similar message: "gentlemanliness involves climbing out of the abyss and putting it resolutely behind one... both [Oliver and David] are gentlemen by birth

reserved for that use, it is not put further in than is necessary..." (22)

Then there are are Joe's awkward struggles with his hat when he comes to London, and we are made to share Pip's embarrassment at Joe's embarrassment:

It [his hat] demanded from him a constant attention, and a quickness of eye and hand, very like that exacted by wicket-keeping. He made extraordinary play with it, and showed the greatest skill; now, rushing at it and catching it neatly as it dropped; now, merely stopping it midway, beating it up, and humouring it in various parts of the room... (27)

A third example is the wonderful scene before Wemmick marries Miss Skiffins:

That discreet damsel was attired as usual except that she was now engaged in substituting for her green kid gloves, a pair of white. The whose tenacious hold on an inner conviction of gentility throughout their sufferings is rewarded by fairy godparents".

In *Great Expectations* the fantasy of fairy godparents and innate gentility is dispensed with utterly. Pip grows up a blacksmith's boy and never turns out to be anything else (we are told nothing about his father); he has to acquire gentility rather than recover it. Miss Havisham is like a grotesque, witch-like version of David Copperfield's Aunt Betsey – her name reinforcing the idea that she is a "sham" – while the source of Pip's money, and eventual gentility, turns out to be another "witch" – Magwitch – who is associated from the beginning with the world of violent crime and who has made

Aged was likewise occupied in preparing a similar sacrifice for the altar of Hymen. The old gentleman, however, experienced so much difficulty in getting his gloves on that Wemmick found it necessary to put him with his back against a pillar, and then to get behind the pillar itself, and pull away at them, while I for my part held the old gentleman round the waist, that he might present an equal and safe resistance. By dint of this ingenious scheme, his gloves were got on to perfection. (55)

The comedy here stems in part from the mock-heroic, mock-epic language, with the references to "damsel" and the "altar of Hymen", the Greek god of marriage, and in part from the brilliant improvisatory comedy – ironically called an "ingenious scheme" – of putting on the old man's gloves. No one but Dickens could have invented this.◆

his money in what is literally the underworld: Australia. There is no attempt in *Great Expectations* to romanticise gentility or to resist or underplay the links between the gentrified life to which Pip aspires and the criminal world into which he could so easily have slipped. Rather, Dickens is concerned to stress how interrelated they are – how one depends upon the other: Pip, after all, is given the financial basis of a comfortable life only to find that it is made possible by someone whose whole history is, in effect, a contradiction of the refinement which he seeks. "Behind every fortune," wrote Balzac, "lies a crime." Similarly, Dickens suggests that gentility presupposes an underclass, and because of the nature of Victorian society an underclass in which, for many belonging to it, there was little choice but to live outside the law.

Great Expectations is Dickens's most compelling analysis of what he had come to think was wrong in his society. It is seen as a society, says Q.D. Leavis,

> that first makes and then executes criminals, with a quite arbitrary conception of justice, a society in which all are therefore guilty inescapably – there are no innocent, only those more or less aware of guilt, ranging from the blindly self-righteous to the repentantly self-accusing.

The notion of universal guilt is central to *Great*

Expectations. In analysing Pip's rise to gentility, Dickens dwells constantly on the misgivings his hero feels, on the personal betrayals he commits and above all on the guilt of which he is always conscious.* While Pip does not discover Magwitch's role in his destiny until he grows up, the secret complicity between them established at the beginning of the novel continues throughout and leaves us, by the end, questioning the very notion of gentility. Pip's great expectations come to nothing; they lead not to happiness but to loneliness and disenchantment, as is evident not just from the tale he tells but from the ironic, remorseful tone in which he tells it. However else it can be described, *Great Expectations* is, ultimately, a novel about lost illusions.

What makes the opening scenes so powerful?

"The distinguishing quality of Dickens's people is that they are solitaries," the novelist V.S. Pritchett observed in 1947. "They are people caught living in a world of their own." Among Dickens's solitary heroes, the most solitary of all is Pip. His narrative begins with him sadly contemplating the gravestones of his mother, father and five (male)

*The novel begins in 1810 and ends with Pip narrating events nearly 50 years later, at the time when the work was first being read.

siblings in a deserted marshland graveyard: cut off from the past by the death of his parents, left only with the harsh guardianship of a single surviving sister, his "first most vivid and broad impression of the identity of things" comes when he is seized by a convict who leaps out from behind the gravestone of his dead father.

"Hold your noise!" cried a terrible voice, as a man started up from among the graves at the side of the church porch. "Keep still, you little devil, or I'll cut your throat!" (1)

Pip's world is literally turned upside down; the convict lifts him up by the ankles, and from this point onwards his whole sense of himself is coloured by his guilty knowledge of this man "who had been soaked in water, and smothered in mud, and lamed by stones, and cut by flints, and stung by nettles, and torn by briars". Dorothy Van Ghent writes of this passage:

The apparition is that of all suffering that the earth can inflict, and that the apparition presents itself to a child is as much to say that every child, whatever its innocence, inherits guilt (as the potential of his acts) for the condition of man. The inversion of natural order begins here with first self-consciousness: the child is heir to the sins of the "fathers".

Dickens brilliantly establishes Pip's sense of guilt in these early pages. It is shown to be inevitable, as if Dickens were anticipating Freud, who argued gloomily in *Civilization and its Discontents* (1930) that the function of society is to make people feel guilty: even if he had not met the convict, Pip has been brought up to believe he has committed a sin simply by being born. The encounter with Magwitch in the churchyard "merely plays in an even harsher key the tune he is used to at home",

EDUCATION

There are two occasions in *Great Expectations* when Magwitch erupts, terrifyingly, into Pip's life: in the opening chapter and, 15 years later, in chapter 39. On both occasions, he is reading. In the graveyard he is attempting to decipher the inscriptions on the gravestones. In the second scene he has been reading self-improvingly, a habit he has strenuously kept up, he informs us, even in the depth of his metropolitan dissipations. "Through good and evil", he piously tells us, "I stuck to my books."

Literacy pops up time and again as a leitmotif of *Great Expectations*. Magwitch's complaints about the disadvantages that have made him a criminal, for example. "Them that writes fifty hand," he says, will always have advantages in life. Miss Havisham's last words are: "Take the pencil and write under my name, as A.L. French neatly puts it. Pip's life is "largely a matter of being threatened, bullied, knocked around, and made to feel ashamed of eating and being alive". When he returns to the forge for Christmas dinner, Mr Hubble (the local wheelwright – hence "hub") calls him "naterally wicious", while Mr Pumblechook says nastily that if he had been born a pig the butcher "would have come up to you as you lay in your straw... and he would have shed your blood and had your life". Pip's sister, Mrs Joe, then complains

'I forgive her'." The last thing Pip does with Magwitch is to read to him.

Teachers figure centrally in *Great Expectations*. The comically worst of them is Mr Wopsle's great-aunt who runs the "dame's school" in which, for tuppence a week, the young Pip picks up an extremely rudimentary grasp of letters. (Dickens himself had attended a dame's school in Chatham, aged six.) Pip describes the *Great Expectations* establishment satirically:

The Educational scheme or Course established by Mr. Wopsle's great-aunt may be resolved into the following synopsis. The pupils ate apples and put straws down one another's backs, until Mr. Wopsle's great-aunt collected her energies, and made an indiscriminate totter at them with a birch-rod. (10)

In London Pip is tutored by a university man, the amiable but ineffectual Matthew Pocket who adds some intellectual polish to his pupil – but the core of the hero's education (like Dickens's) is the result of his private reading.◆

of the trouble he has been to her:

> [She] entered on a fearful catalogue of all the
> illnesses I had been guilty of, and all the acts of
> sleeplessness I had committed, and all the high
> places I had tumbled from, and all the low places
> I had tumbled into, and all the injuries I had
> done myself, and all the times she had wished me
> in my grave, and I had contumaciously refused
> to go there. (4)

As A.L. French notes in his essay, "Beating and
Cringing", Pip's ironic narrative tone often works
to muffle the meaning of what he is saying: here,
for example, the bouncing rhythm of "all the... all
the" makes it hard to grasp that what Mrs Joe is
doing here is publicly, and over Christmas dinner,
expressing the appalling thought that she wishes
Pip were dead. It is with similar facetiousness that
Pip tells us he is given only the most horrible
scraps of meat – "those obscure corners of pork of
which the pig, when living, had had the least
reason to be vain".

Now, in his first conscious moment in life –
there is a kind of rebirth in the churchyard – Pip
finds that compounding his natural sense of guilt
is the knowledge that he too must turn criminal,
forced to commit the crime of stealing food from
his sister, and a file from Joe, her husband. With
no one to confide in, and knowing Joe cannot

protect him from his sister, he has no choice but to do as the convict demands, and his child's sense of fear and guilt is cleverly evoked by Dickens in deft touches: the way the natural features of the landscape appear to run at Pip when he returns to the marshes – with even the cattle looking at him accusingly – and his fevered imaginings before he steals the pork pie:

> As soon as the great black velvet pall outside my little window was shot with grey, I got up and went downstairs; every board upon the way, and every crack in every board, calling after me, "Stop thief!" and "Get up, Mrs Joe!" In the pantry, which was far more abundantly supplied than usual, owing to the season, I was very much alarmed by a hare hanging up by the heels, whom I rather thought I caught, when my back was half turned, winking. (2)

The hare hanging by the heels echoes Pip's experience with the convict and reminds us that hanging, not by the heels but by the neck, is the all-too-likely fate of those who turn to crime. But there is no turning back: the crime Pip commits, and his sympathy for the starving convict he helps – a sympathy made even more resonant given that it is Christmas Day – creates a bond between them which cannot be broken. This bond is shown with great economy by Dickens:

Pitying his desolation, and watching him as he gradually settled down upon the pie, I made bold to say, "I am glad you enjoy it."'

"Did you speak?"

"I said, I was glad you enjoyed it."'

"Thankee, my boy. I do" (3)

The repetition underlines the point, says Q.D. Leavis:

the convict is not only "my" convict to Pip, Pip has now become "his" boy. And Pip can never

THE MARSHES

"Ours was the marsh country, down by the river" Pip says (1). The county is Kent. The original for the churchyard of chapter 1 may be Cooling, between Gravesend and Rochester, which is next-door to Chatham. Dickens lived at Ordnance Terrace in Chatham from 1817 to 1822 – the house still stands – and knew the area thoroughly, and of course moved back near there when he bought a house at Gad's Hill. Satis House must be in Rochester (perhaps based on Restoration House there). Cooling Churchyard has the gravestones of 12 children who died in infancy, surrounding the graves of their parents. Rochester, on the Medway river, is 30 miles from London, but the river Dickens means is the Thames, flowing out into the North Sea. ◆

again feel the separation from the criminal that is felt by the consciously self-righteous, a fellow-feeling that is kept alive by Dickens throughout the first half of the novel.

Part of this is natural sympathy for a hunted outcast, part of it guilty knowledge, a knowledge kept alive by a series of events which Pip later recognises, when thinking of Newgate, as "this taint of prison and crime... starting out like a stain" and which makes him, for instance, think the sergeant he runs into when he gets home, holding out handcuffs, has come to arrest him.

The encounter in the graveyard which is Pip's first fully conscious experience is important, too, in establishing the element of violence and animality which runs through the novel. The convict, Magwitch – a "fearful man... with a great iron on his leg... no hat, and with broken shoes" – is seen as close to being a wild animal in human form, inseparable from the savage landscape out of which he erupts. "I wish I was a frog," he says, as Pip leaves. "Or a eel." He terrifies Pip by talking like a cannibal – "You young dog... what fat cheeks you ha' got... Darn me if I couldn't eat 'em" – and describing a (fictional) young accomplice who has "a secret way, pecooliar to himself, of getting at a boy, and at his heart, and at his liver" and who could "tear [Pip] open". (We do not need Freud to remind us that Magwitch is allegorising something subhuman in himself.) When he is brought food, he gulps it furtively, like a dog. "No other work of Dickens, not even *Oliver Twist* or *Our Mutual Friend*, is so impregnated with violence, latent and actual, or so imaginatively aware of the gradations between the primitive and the refined," says Robin Gilmour.

Pip, at home, has to endure his sister's "hard and heavy hand", random thrashings from Tickler and unpleasant doses of tarwater which make him conscious of "going about, smelling like a new fence". Mrs Joe's system of bringing up by hand – demeaning, savage, brutalising – is the regime of a primitive rural society depending almost exclusively on physical discipline and not at all on the development of mind and spirit, exacerbating Pip's sense of guilt and leaving him timid and self-conscious. Everyone bar Joe conspires to make Pip feel he is scarcely better than a young animal: punched and beaten and scrubbed by his sister and bullied by Pumblechook, he is soon to be despised by Estella who slaps his face and calls him a "little coarse monster" and to have his hair poked into his eyes by Mr Wopsle. "Pip's encounter with Magwitch brings to dramatic focus all the violence, the injustice, the physical and moral coercion inherent in his environment," says Gilmour. "Never has any novel been so imbued with the horrors of infancy," says the biographer and critic Peter Ackroyd. Pip is robbed of all dignity; he is a child alone in a society of adults, sustained only by Joe's affection and a deep sense of outrage and injustice. (He longs to pull Wopsle's nose and to fight back against Pumblechook.)

And we watch it all, as it were, through two sets of eyes: one mature, one juvenile. It was happening then; it is happening now. Pip's narrative voice, though frequently laced with irony and humour, combines in passages such as the one which opens the novel a sense of emotional immediacy with the kind of calm pictorial composition that only a mature sensibility could achieve. It is an extraordinary mixed effect which is peculiar to *Great Expectations*; the unique tone which Dickens achieves is one found nowhere else in his work.

Is Pip a snob?

Dickens held no brief for village life. He is essentially an urban novelist, with none of the sense of the compensating benefits or attractions of provincial existence one finds in, say, George Eliot's *Silas Marner* or *Adam Bede*. The opening scenes of *Great Expectations* make it vividly clear why Pip has few qualms about quitting the forge when he has the chance to advance his prospects in London, and these scenes need to be borne in mind when considering the familiar charge that

Great Expectations is a "snob's progress" – and that Pip would have been better staying where he was. Much of the energy of Dickens's writing in the early part of the novel is devoted to showing just how mean and constricted Pip's circumstances are, and how understandable his wish to escape them. It is a theme later developed by Dickens's admirer, Thomas Hardy, in *Jude the Obscure*.

The charge that Pip is a snob is so frequently made as to have become a kind of shorthand label for the novel: reviewing the BBC's 2011 adaptation (its fifth), for example, Anne Billson in *The Daily Telegraph* referred to the book as "Dickens's *Bildungsroman* about an upwardly mobile young man blinkered by snobbery", an interpretation admittedly made more plausible by a script which played up this aspect of Dickens's story. The charge was aired most forcefully by the critic Humphry House in his revisionary 1960 monograph, *The Dickens World*. Labelling *Great Expectations* a "snob's progress", House asserts that Pip's behaviour is pretentious and his self-improvement shallow. "It comes to little more than accent, table manners and clothes." Clothes, the proverb may claim, "maketh the man". They do not, House insists, make the gentleman. Pip reads books, grants House, but we are never told what books and we can assume they are nothing like the ones an undergraduate would be reading at one of the two great universities. Pip, at the end of his career, is still what Estella called him at the beginning: "common". It is merely that the commonness is more expensively garbed. He is not a gentleman but a "gent": no more the real thing than Wemmick's castle is Blenheim Palace.

House's disapproving opinion of Pip finds some confirmation in the very complex way Dickens presents his hero – or, to put it more exactly, in the way the older Pip presents the younger Pip. When, for example, after coming into his "expectations", he is pursued through the streets of Rochester by Trabb's boy, the tailor's assistant, Pip is mortified by the boy's behaviour. The boy behaves like a kind of satirical alter ego, mocking Pip for his new-found status:

> *[He] was strutting along the pavement...*
> *attended by a company of delighted young*
> *friends to whom he from time to time exclaimed,*
> *with a wave of his hand, "Don't know yah!"*
> *Words cannot state the amount of aggravation*
> *and injury wreaked upon me by Trabb's boy;*
> *when passing abreast of me, he pulled up his*
> *shirt-collar, twined his side-hair, stuck an arm*
> *akimbo, and smirked extravagantly by, wriggling*
> *his elbows and body, and drawling to his*
> *attendants, "Don't know yah, don't know yah,*
> *'pon my soul don't know yah!" (30)*

What this passage may be thought to reveal,

however, is less Pip's snobbery than his hyper-sensitivity. He is uneasily aware that he is not quite the genuine article, as this episode and many others suggest. (Drummle is particularly adept at rubbing this raw spot.) He knows he will never match his friend Herbert in grace and style: "he [Herbert] had that frank and easy way with him which was very taking" (22); he expressed "in every look and tone, a natural incapacity to do anything secret and mean"; "he carried off his rather old clothes much better than I carried off my new suit".

The argument that *Great Expectations* is a "snob's progress" is incisively and comprehensively countered by Q.D. Leavis in what is perhaps the most influential essay ever written on Dickens's novel. In her provokingly entitled "How we must

DICKENS AND CLASS

The gaudiness of Dickens's waistcoats was often remarked on as something – well, not *comme il faut*. He did not, it was felt, have that instinctive sartorial taste which would have come naturally to a man born in a higher station of life. "All very well," sighed Fitzjames Stephen about *Oliver Twist*, "but damned low." So too, one apprehends, was the author of *Oliver Twist* "low". Sad, given his manifest genius, but true.

It wasn't quite a sneer. It was more a tactful acknowledgement by those who never themselves had to read *Great Expectations"* – must? – she argues that Humphry House and critics who see the book as he does are simply "unable to appreciate the delicacy, subtlety and intention of Dickens's searching investigation into Pip's feelings, successfully presented in all their complexity and psychological truth". Those who label Pip a snob fail to understand how someone like him would have felt in the early 19th century, or Dickens's own belief both that, in Leavis's words, "there was a respectable content in the idea of a gentleman" and that Pip "did well to leave behind him the limitations of the village and the vulgar little world of the market town, as Dickens saw them".

It may be true that Mrs Leavis's own situation made her unusually sensitive to Pip's plight. Brought up strictly in the Jewish faith, she fell in

struggle that acquiring "class" is neither easy nor quickly done and for many of us better never attempted if we want a happy life. Dickens never quite mastered English grammar, complained the Winchester-educated Anthony Trollope. It would have been so much better had he attended a public school and had Cicero drummed into him.

Shakespeare, with Jonson's comment about "little Latin and less Greek", was subjected to the same condescension.

Dickens had a series of feuds during his professional life with a fellow novelist, public school-educated William Makepeace Thackeray. Class was as much at the root of their quarrels as professional rivalry. ◆

love – with one of the 20th century's most eminent literary critics, F.R. Leavis – and "married out". So aggrieved were her family that they had the service of the dead read out for her, in effect casting her out. Whether or not this made her more sympathetic to Pip's self-transformation, she is surely right that Dickens

> didn't share the lip service now given to the idea of equality, which he detested when he saw it operating in America and satirised in *Martin Chuzzlewit*; and the reluctance in our day of critics to believe this, or to believe sincerely in the existence of any distinctions save those based on money, must not prevent us from recognising that for Dickens class distinctions were valid since ideally they represented an aspiration towards distinction and fineness.

It is worth noting, too, that whereas Dickens does not actually use the word "snob" in *Great Expectations*, it was certainly current, and used by others – notably Thackeray, who writes witheringly about a variety of toadies in his *Book of Snobs* (1848) – and there are certainly snobs in the novel, even if they are not described as such: Pumblechook and Mrs Pocket are blinded to all other human considerations by wealth and social position. Pip, one should remember, is very quick to see through both.

*John Mills (left) as Pip and Alec Guinness as Herbert Pocket
in David Lean's 1946 film adaptation*

None of this is to excuse all Pip's behaviour. His treatment of Joe and Biddy has been attacked by many critics, and rightly. He behaves badly, even disgracefully, especially to Joe. But what choice does he have? Is it realistic to believe he could have done anything else?

Joe represents everything that is best about life in rural Kent: he is gentle and affectionate, and his constancy and generosity to Pip help mitigate the worst excesses of the dreadful Mrs Joe (never given a first name since this might make her seem more sympathetic). He is associated from the beginning with the fire and the forge – we first see him poking the fire and early on he shields Pip from Mrs Joe's wrath in the chimney-corner: in the novel's symbolism, says Robin Gilmour, the fire and the forge "are the source of positive, life-giving energies, opposed to the 'extinguished fires' of the defunct brewery in the sterile Satis House" – though fire also eventually destroys Satis House and its mistress: Dickens's symbolism was rarely simple.

Originally conceived by Dickens as "good-natured" and "foolish", Joe grows in stature to become the "gentle Christian man", whom Pip blesses in his illness and recognises as possessing a "great nature" – a nature which Pip betrays in pursuit of his expectations. As Gilmour says, however, "it is in the nature of Pip's effort to cultivate himself that it should involve a betrayal of Joe"; he could not have escaped the forge without such a betrayal.

Gentle and affectionate he may be, but Joe is also limited and moreover, in his effort to preserve domestic harmony, does little to protect Pip from Mrs Joe's "rampages", much less, as Pip is aware, than he could do. Joe's limitations, and his inadequacy as a father figure, are exposed in the theft of the food and the file. Pip feels he ought to tell Joe about the deed, but knows he can't.

It was much upon my mind (particularly when I first saw him looking about for the file) that I ought to tell Joe the whole truth. Yet I did not, and for the reason that I mistrusted that if I did, he would think me worse than I was. The fear of losing Joe's confidence, and of thenceforth sitting in the chimney-corner at night staring drearily at my forever lost companion and friend, tied up my tongue. (6)

Pip is quite right about this, as soon becomes evident. After his first visit to Satis House, the great turning point in his life, he is eagerly interrogated by Pumblechook and his sister about what happened there:

"Now, boy! What was she a doing of, when you went in today?" asked Mr. Pumblechook.
"She was sitting," I answered, "in a black

velvet coach."

Mr. Pumblechook and Mrs. Joe stared at one another – as they well might – and both repeated, "In a black velvet coach?"

"Yes," said I. "And Miss Estella – that's her niece, I think – handed her in cake and wine at the coach-window, on a gold plate. And we all had cake and wine on gold plates. And I got up behind the coach to eat mine, because she told me to.

"Was anybody else there?" asked Mr. Pumblechook.

"Four dogs... and they fought for veal-cutlets out of a silver basket." (9)

George Orwell was charmed by this episode. Pip, he says, "finding himself completely unable to describe what he has seen",

takes refuge in a series of outrageous lies – which, of course, are eagerly believed. All the isolation of childhood is there. And how accurately [Dickens] has recorded the mechanisms of the child's mind, its visualising tendency, its sensitiveness to certain kinds of impression.

This is true enough. But it also – in parodic fashion – foretells the grand things which, even at this embryonic stage of his life, Pip "expects".

When Pip later hears his sister relate the story to Joe, and find that he too proves credulous, the young fantasist is "overtaken by penitence... Towards Joe, and Joe only, I considered myself a young monster." The realisation that Joe is as easily taken in as his sister and that his horizon is equally limited, appears, in Robin Gilmour's words,

> a terrible betrayal of the one source of love and trust in Pip's life; and it has the effect of cutting him off from the simple morality of the forge and isolating him still further in his own consciousness.

Matters are made even worse when Pip tells Joe the truth and finds that Joe, far from seeing it as harmless fantasy reflecting a boy's confused state of mind, considers it as downright lying: "a sincere well-wisher would adwise, Pip, their [the lies] being dropped into your meditations, when you go upstairs to bed," he says sententiously. All Joe's reaction achieves, of course, is to make Pip feel even more guilty and anxious to escape. This has little to do with snobbery; nor does Pip's embarrassed reaction when Joe pays an early visit to Miss Havisham and behaves impossibly – he is never comfortable anywhere except at the forge. The anguish Pip suffers over this meeting, says Mrs Leavis, is what anyone in the circumstances at his age must have felt. Dickens indeed makes us feel it with him.

Pip himself, the mature recorder of his own exemplary history, does not deal tenderly with himself, recording mercilessly every least attractive impulse, but we should notice that these are mitigated always by generous misgivings, permeated by uneasy self-criticism, and contrary movements of feeling of a self-corrective kind.

Pip does not mean – never means – to drop Joe; on the contrary, he endeavours at first to help Joe and to fit him for "a higher sphere", attempting, without success, to teach him to read and feeling aggrieved when Biddy says that Joe will never go along with his plans. As time runs out before he is due to leave, Pip becomes, as he himself puts it, "more and more appreciative of the society of Joe and Biddy" (19); the night before he leaves he "had an impulse to go down again and entreat Joe to walk with me in the morning. I did not." Through all this Pip makes clear he was at the time "aware of my own ingratitude" – not the kind of thought one associates with a snob – and almost leaves the coach to walk home for another evening there. In the circumstances, as a number of critics suggested, few of us could be confident of acquitting ourselves better. Pip is separated from the forge not just by what is bad about it, but by what is good too: Joe's simple code of living is as frustrating to his youthful intelligence, curiosity and sympathy – what he calls his "pitying young fancy" – as Mrs Joe's nastiness. But cutting himself off from Joe's love as he becomes more self-aware is a source of constant painful remorse.

While Pip himself might have been inclined to endorse Humphry House's verdict of his social pretensions, it grossly oversimplifies Dickens's art to call *Great Expectations* a "snob's progress". It does justice neither to the complexity and subtlety of Dickens's story, nor to the way it is told.

Charles Dickens, circa 1867-8

Why does Pip feel so drawn to Satis House?

Unlike some Victorians, Dickens never romanticises the notion of self-improvement. In his famous, best-selling manual, *Self-Help* (1859), Samuel Smiles argues that "every man's first duty is, to improve, to educate, to elevate himself". The process of self-improvement, he says, should not be undertaken to bring worldly wealth so much as to strengthen character and give the individual a sense of dignity and independence. A critic of snobbery, he argues that the "True Gentleman" is essentially classless: "The inbred politeness which springs from right-heartedness and kindly feeling is of no exclusive rank or station."

In the real Victorian world, however, it was not so easy to turn oneself into a gentleman without becoming involved in questions of class, a fact of which Dickens was well aware: for all Smiles's disclaimers, Dickens knew that that the impulse to improve was usually fuelled, if not inspired, by social and sexual ambitions. It is no accident that Pip inherits his fortune rather than having to make it himself: Dickens wanted his hero to enjoy the "rewards" of self-improvement without having to work for them; that way, he could concentrate on the social and sexual implications, and the inherent paradoxes of the self-improvement idea. From the moment of his first visit to Satis House,

CRITICS ON
GREAT EXPECTATIONS

66 *Great Expectations: Alliance between atmosphere and plot (the convicts) make it more solid and satisfactory than anything else of Dickens known to me* 99
E.M. Forster, in his notebook, 1925

66 *Dickens did in fact know that Great Expectations was his most compactly perfect book* 99
George Bernard Shaw, 1937

66 *Psychologically, the latter part of Great Expectations is about the best thing Dickens ever did* 99
George Orwell, 1948

66 *Snobbery is not a crime. Why should Pip feel like a criminal?* 99
Julian Moynahan, 1960

66 *The most important things about Great Expectations are also the most obvious – a fact that is fortunate for the book but unfortunate for the critic* 99
Christopher Ricks, 1962

66 *To read Great Expectations is, first of all, to listen to it* 99
David Gervais, 1984

Pip's desire to improve himself is caught up with sexual and social fantasies.

At Satis House, Pip's feelings of guilt and moral confusion are at the same time compounded by a sense of shame: Miss Havisham and Estella make him feel inadequate; his hands, he learns, are coarse and his boots too thick. Estella treats him with disdain – "He calls the knaves Jacks, this boy!" she says as they play cards (8), and she dumps his dinner on the ground "as if I were a dog in disgrace", an especially humiliating gesture in that it reminds Pip of the way his convict ate like a

THE ORIGINAL MISS HAVISHAM

Miss Havisham had a real world original. In 1853 Dickens wrote an essay in his paper, *Household Words*, about a strange woman he recalled seeing in his childhood, wandering around Oxford Street, in London. "The White Woman" was her nickname.

She was dressed entirely in white, with a ghastly white plaiting round her head and face, inside her white bonnet ...with white boots she picks her way through winter dirt... she was a conceited old creature, cold and formal in manner, and evidently went simpering and on personal grounds alone - no doubt because a wealthy Quaker wouldn't marry her. This is her bridal dress.

The woman in white – and his childhood disgust for

dog. A boy of only seven or eight, Pip can't help but be impressed by his new surroundings. For all her unpleasantness, Estella and Satis House offer an undreamt-of alternative to the "dull endurance" and "flat colour" of his life in the marshes: "whoever had this house," he thinks, "could want nothing else". He is determined to become worthy of Estella and sets out to educate himself *before* becoming aware that he has any "expectations". Suddenly, his life is enriched:

What could I become with these surroundings?

her – stuck in his mind for 50 years.

Estella too had an "original" in the real world – Ellen ("Nellie" – the echo with "Estella" is significant) Ternan, the young actress he had fallen in love with and for whom he had broken up his marriage. The rudimentary facts about Ellen, Dickens's "Invisible Woman", are well known – but little else is. She was born 28 years later than Dickens, into an acting family. Dickens first saw her, aged 18, when she was on the stage acting in a performance he himself had funded. The 45-year-old novelist fell in love with her. He promptly removed his wife of 22 years, Kate, the mother of his ten children, from their home with the (wholly Dickensian) explanation that she was "dull". The truth is, as Dickens's latest biographer Claire Tomalin argues, his wife had lost the allure which he, a powerfully sexed and emotionally ruthless man of 46, required. After 1859, as he began to write *Great Expectations*, Charles Dickens was a bachelor again.◆

How could my character fail to be influenced
by them? (12)

Dickens shows here, as he does elsewhere in his
work, his belief in the imaginative life, in the need
everyone feels to have something to live for
beyond day-to-day realities. Satis House – the
name, literally 'Enough House', "meant more than
it said", says Estella – reflects Pip's thoughts.
Enough is never enough.

Whenever I watched the vessels standing out to
sea with their white sails spread, I somehow
thought of Miss Havisham and Estella... Miss
Havisham and Estella and that strange house and
the strange life appeared to have something to do
with everything that was picturesque. (15)

Satis House, then, comes to symbolise for Pip
"everything that was picturesque"; it captures his
imagination because it is the opposite of what he
has known on the marshes. Yet try as he does to
keep the two worlds separate he can never do so:
on his second visit to Satis House, the smoke from
the dining room fire reminds him of "our own
marsh mist" (11), just as on his first visit the
cobwebs on Miss Havisham's bridal cake recall
the damp of the hedges, like "a coarser sort of
spiders' webs" (3), on the morning when he sneaks
food out to Magwitch.

More significantly, Bentley Drummle, who eventually marries Estella, is like an upper-class equivalent of Orlick, a comparison brought home to us in chapter 43, when Pip sees Drummle through a window, "seizing his horse's mane, and mounting in his brutal manner". The "slouching shoulders and ragged hair of this man, whose back was towards me," writes Pip, "reminded me of Orlick". The name Bentley Drummle, with its combination of "bend", "drum" and "pummel" implies his tendency to violence; his function in the scheme of the novel, as Robin Gilmour puts it, is "to remind us that violence and brutality are not confined to life on the marshes" but also exist "in the supposedly refined society of London".

Estella's marriage to Drummle is an important clue to her character. This "proud and refined" girl, the incarnation, for Pip, of the civilised life, can prefer Drummle to him because there exists in her a violent animal nature to which Pip is blind. We know this already, from the fight in which Pip beats Herbert – "the pale young gentleman" – at their first meeting in chapter 11. Unseen by either of them, Estella is watching and when she comes down to Pip afterwards "there was a bright flush upon her face, as though something had happened to delight her". She offers to let him kiss her, and he does, and while he feels "the kiss was given to the coarse common boy as a piece of money might have been, and that it was worth nothing", it is more significant than that; it goes to the heart of what Gilmour calls "the supreme paradox" of Pip's life: "Estella can only respond to him when he exhibits those qualities of physical force and animal aggression which, in order to win her, he is at pains to civilise out of himself."

Gentility, the novel suggests, involves alienation and repression; it means, for Pip, cutting himself off from the vital energy and warm instinctive life symbolised by the fire at the forge. Indeed, immediately after describing the "bright flush" on Estella's face, Pip tells us how, on his walk home, he sees in the distance "Joe's furnace... flinging a path of fire across the road".

How real is Pip's love for Estella?

Why does Pip love Estella? One answer is that he doesn't; she, after all, is utterly indifferent to him; he is never happy in her company; his feelings about her are always absurd and unrealistic; what he loves is not her but what she represents; she is the embodiment of his aspirations.

But Dickens suggests there is more to it than that. The whole pattern of the novel is one of relationships based round violence. Giving his opinion of Bentley Drummle before she marries Estella in chapter 48, Jaggers says: "A fellow like our friend the Spider... either beats, or cringes. He may cringe and growl, or cringe and not growl; but he either beats or cringes. Ask Wemmick *his* opinion." Wemmick's opinion is the same. It is an opinion the novel itself also seems to endorse.

Most of the main characters of *Great Expectations* can be put into one, or sometimes both, of Jaggers's categories. Beating is a constant in the book. The song Pip sings at the forge and to Miss Havisham makes it almost a part of everyday life: "Beat it out, Old Clem"; Orlick is beaten by Joe in a fight, then beats Mrs Joe, who is herself a beater. But when she has been battered by Orlick, she cringes to him, as Molly cringes to Jaggers. *Great Expectations,* it might be said, is a rare exercise in thinking about sadism and masochism in human relationships, relationships between parent and child as well as those between adults.

Perhaps the only parent–child relationship in the book that is normal is the one between Wemmick and his Aged P, but that, as A.L. French points out, exists behind a raised drawbridge and, besides, the Aged P is stone-deaf so can't really communicate with his son, nor his son with him. There is even the implication, says French, that affection in human relationships "may depend on *not* communicating".

Pip's sensibility is fixed early; he is a kisser of rods, or, in Jaggers's phrase, a "cringer", and it's not hard to see why: tyrannised for years by his there's something in Joe that enjoys being dominated," says French, "there is no less something in Pip which feels drawn to Estella for the very reason that she ill-treats him".

Joe's own background is important. He is, he tells Pip, the son of a drunk who stopped him from going to school and "hammered" him and his mother; his image of his mother is of a woman "drudging and slaving and breaking her honest hart and never getting no peace in her mortal days". He doesn't want to put Mrs Joe in the position of his mother, or, as he puts it, "I'm dead afeard of going

SEX IN *GREAT EXPECTATIONS*

Victorian fiction was notoriously constrained in its dealings with sex. It could not, as Dickens noted satirically, "bring a blush to the maiden cheek". Henry James described the constraint more bluntly. The novelist of this period was subject, he said, to the "tyranny of the young reader".

Sex had to be smuggled in, via hints and codes. Dickens was a past master in the necessary techniques of introducing sex without seeming to be writing about it, or offending the maiden cheek. Mrs Joe's violence against men, for example - all those threatening pins in her apron - may be read as what D.H. Lawrence would call "sex gone bad". She and Joe have no children – why? He has one, promptly enough, when he marries Biddy.

Is the 40-year-old Pip, in

mother, or, as he puts it, "I'm dead afeard of going wrong in the way or not doing what's right by a woman". (7) So he relives his parents' marriage though in reverse: this time it is the man who gets no peace and the woman who does the hammering. And if Joe can really believe that his father was good at heart, as he says he does, then he can also believe, and make Pip believe, that his wife, Mrs Joe, is "a fine figure of a woman". Pip's reaction to this bit of autobiography is curious and, as French says, significant. "Young as I was, I believe that I dated a new admiration of Joe from that night..." It

that last scene with Estella in the ruined garden in Satis House, as virginal as he was when he first went there, 30 years before? Hints buried deep in the text suggest that Pip may not have kept the temple of his body entirely pure. When, for example, Wemmick warns "Don't Go Home" – because their rooms are being watched by the police - he spends the night in a private room at the Hummums (Turkish baths) in Covent Garden (favourite resort of ladies of the night). Then, as now, the bath-house was a place of "assignation": where a young man could privately enjoy illicit pleasures of the night – with either sex. Dickens could as easily have had Pip stay at some discreet hotel. But he wanted, we feel, to tell his adult readers something.

One of the interesting new lines of approach which have opened up in Dickensian criticism in recent years is "queer theory". Theorists pursuing this line have found a rich quarry in *Great Expectations*. Orlick's grabbing Pip in the lime kiln, with the intention of soon killing him, has – queer theorists note – meaningfully erotic as is an admiration which the older narrating Pip seems to approve of – there is no hint, anyway, that he *disapproves* of it – and from now on Pip goes through life as Joe does: allowing himself to be dominated. Only once, when he knocks Herbert down in their boxing match, does he square up to life, but in this instance he has no choice.

There is no reason to disbelieve Pip, then, when he tells us in chapter 29 that he finds Estella "irresistible" and loves her "against all reason, against promise, against peace, against hope, against happiness, against all discouragement that

well as homicidal overtones:

> *Not only were my arms pulled close to my sides, but the pressure on my bad arm caused me exquisite pain. Sometimes, a strong man's hand, sometimes a strong man's breast, was set against my mouth to deaden my cries, and with a hot breath always close to me, I struggled ineffectually in the dark, while I was fastened tight to the wall. "And now," said the suppressed voice with another oath, "call out again, and I'll make short work of you!" (53)*

Is this man-on-man assault or quasi rape? It is, whatever one's chosen analysis, the only close carnal embrace depicted in the novel. Contrast it, for example, with the genteel (gloved) hand-holding of Pip and Estella, in the last chapter of the novel. There is no "hot breath" or "breasts on mouths" in that frigid exchange. Which of the two encounters has a higher sexual charge? Is there a sexual element in Orlick's lifelong stalking of Pip? The language (e.g. "exquisite pain") suggests something along those lines.◆

could be". Dickens, says A.L. French,

> clearly relates Pip's feelings for Estella's
> "irresistibility" to his early impressions and to
> his consequent tendency to enjoy being hurt...
> It's not merely that he loves Estella although
> she isn't "human perfection" or anything like it;
> he loves her precisely because she is more like
> the reverse and, as she frankly implies herself, is,
> in her lack of normal affections, scarcely human
> at all.

The love Pip feels, indeed, is the love Miss Havisham orders him to feel:

> *"I'll tell you", said she, in the same hurried*
> *passionate whisper, "what real love is. It is*
> *blind devotion, unquestioning self-humiliation,*
> *utter submission, trust and belief against*
> *yourself and against the whole world giving*
> *up your whole heart and soul to the smiter –*
> *as I did!" (12)*

Estella has been brought up by Miss Havisham to take revenge on men, and thus Pip is cast in the role of victim, "confirming him in the part he has always played". Hopelessly in thrall to Estella, and to his parent-substitute Miss Havisham, Pip shamefully neglects Joe, failing to visit him at the forge

> *because I knew she would be contemptuous of*

*him. It was but a day gone, and Joe had brought
the tears into my eyes; they had soon dried, God
forgive me! soon dried. (29)*

The relationship between Pip and Estella goes on
as it begins. "I suffered every kind and degree of
torture that Estella could cause me," he writes in
chapter 38; she teases him and slights him and
though he realises his own perversity – "I never
had one hour's happiness in her society" – it
makes no difference: love, to Pip, simply *is* "every
kind and degree of torture".

The extent to which Pip invites suffering is
clear in one vivid early scene, says the feminist
critic Hilary Schor. He stands at the door of the
forge with Joe on a "dry cold night", reflecting that
this is a night when a man lying out on the
marshes would die.

*...then I looked at the stars, and considered how
awful it would be for a man to turn his face up to
them as he froze to death, and see no help or pity
in all the glittering multitude. (7)*

Pip's ability to imagine the man's "awful" fate
suggests his readiness to see himself in the same
position. Schor writes:

It is as if he is choosing his future by choosing his
perspective, choosing to live out the role of

solitary victim, defined by those things more distant, contemplating his own contemplation of them and his inability to reach them or even read them. At this moment, he is a boy looking for a glittering star; he is looking to freeze to death.

The star he finds, of course, is Estella, a girl whose name means "star", and whose "light", we are told on Pip's first visit to Satis House, is seen coming along "the long dark passage like a star". Schor is not sympathetic to Pip – he is, "as everyone knows... an insufferable young man", shallower and more narcissistic than Estella (and more "feminised" too) – and thinks that Estella's scorn, like that of the distant, uncaring stars, *is* her attraction; Pip loves in her "the image of his own expectations, the image of his own desolation, the image of his own destruction".

There are certainly clear and disturbing parallels between Pip and Miss Havisham, who eventually finds out that Estella no more loves her than she does Pip. Miss Havisham, we are told, is "dreadfully" fond of Estella; she hangs on Estella's beauty, words and gestures "and sat mumbling her own trembling fingers while she looked at her, as though she were devouring the beautiful creature she had reared". (38) Pip may not mumble like Miss Havisham, but his love, too, is "dreadful" and "devours" him.

Great Expectations suggests that we can

become emotionally frozen in early life, unable to develop or change. This is precisely what happens to Miss Havisham. Sometimes dismissed as a fairytale witch or a mere adornment – Mrs Leavis calls her a "picturesque convenience" – she is in fact, says A.L. French, "the most striking of the many striking images Dickens finds of emotional arrest".

In this case, the arrest is a deliberate and conscious adult decision – a way of taking revenge on a world "that has let one down, while in fact taking revenge on oneself for one's inadequacy, the inadequacy consisting of having *been* let down". Arguably, it is Miss Havisham's self-destructiveness which Dickens is showing when Pip, in his hallucination in chapter 8, sees her "hanging... by the neck" from "a great wooden beam" in the deserted brewery, as though she had committed suicide – which, in a sense, she has. Herbert Pocket later tells Pip, in chapter 22, that "she was a spoilt child" whose mother died "when she was a baby" and whose father "denied her nothing" – which helps explain why she is so affected when Compeyson jilts her. When she gets Compeyson's letter, normal life for her stops, and she trains Estella to do to men what he has done to her, while training Pip to be to Estella what she has been to Compeyson.

Her success in this shows when Pip visits Satis House in chapter 38:

The candles that lighted that room of hers were placed in sconces on the wall. They were high from the ground, and they burnt with the steady dullness of artificial light in air that is seldom renewed. As I looked round at them, and at the pale gloom they made, and at the stopped clock, and at the withered articles of bridal dress upon the table and the ground, and at her own awful figure with its ghostly reflection thrown large by the fire upon the ceiling and the wall, I saw in everything the construction that my mind had come to, repeated and thrown back to me. (38)

Pip is seeing here not just the effect Miss Havisham has had on herself but also the effect she has had on him. Just as she has stopped herself, like the clocks, so Pip, too, has been "arrested in the earliest state of his 'love'", as French puts it, and the "withered articles of bridal dress" suggest what a marriage to Estella might be like. Pip's capacity for normal feelings is warped by his childhood – he is a "cringer" not a "beater" – and whatever remains of it is destroyed by Miss Havisham and Estella. By the time the latter marries Bentley Drummle, Pip himself has in effect been laid to waste, like Satis House.

What is the significance of Magwitch?

Pip has been harshly judged for his reaction on finally discovering that his patron is not Miss Havisham but Magwitch. Why, asks Ross H. Dabney, does he "recoil in horror" from Magwitch? "Pip's horror is not openly explained, although there is the suggestion that it is founded on the connection established between criminality and his own fortune." Christopher Ricks thinks Pip behaves not just strangely but badly.

The righteous indignation of these critics is odd given the pains Dickens takes in the novel to show precisely why Pip would recoil in horror from such a revelation. Not to sympathise with his "sickened sensations" is profoundly to misunderstand the novel, protests Q.D. Leavis. Modern critics tend to share her view. Pip's reaction is far from simply being one of genteel squeamishness about Magwitch's eating habits and manners, though Dickens's evocation of his personality and speech – "there was Convict in the very grain of the man" (40) – is brilliantly sustained. It reflects his sudden awareness that everything he has believed, and striven for, is an illusion: he has never known Magwitch as anything other than a violent criminal; his hopes had all been that his benefactor was Miss Havisham, a lady (in his eyes); all the facts, as he saw them, seemed to suggest it.*

Now, in an instant, his hopes are dashed. He has no claim on Estella at all. How can he possibly offer to her a father-in-law like this? He has been plucked from his life at the forge and condemned to an uneasy, purposeless life in London – part of his patron's stipulation being that he should not need to earn his own living. At a stroke, and just as he is going peacefully to bed, his efforts have come to nothing. Moreover, it is quickly clear to Pip that Magwitch's bequest has been made less from gratitude than as a way of getting his revenge on

*The facts which didn't, such as the overheard conversation on the stagecoach between two of Magwitch's fellow convicts, were ignored.

THE CRIMINAL CODE

As a child Dickens had himself seen the "hulks" – prison ships – lying in the mouth of the Medway. The prisons, after the Napoleonic Wars and the crime wave that followed, were full to overflowing and decommissioned Royal Navy vessels were used as a temporary measure to hold prisoners, prior to transportation to the colonies – principally Australia. They were dangerous and inhumane places of confinement.

As the Newgate chapters in *Great Expectations* suggest, Dickens was, in principle, in favour of prison reform. He did not believe in cruel and inhumane society. (Vengeance, of course, is also the motive of Estella's patron.) Magwitch, or Provis, behaves as if he owns Pip, turning the ring, which he has paid for, on Pip's finger, taking the watch out of his pocket and demanding to be read foreign languages.

When I complied he, not comprehending a single word would stand before the fire surveying me with the air of an Exhibitor. (40)

Pip realises that, in effect, he has been bought and paid for. As Leavis says, even assuming Estella would ever have him, he can't support her without Magwitch's money, which he can't now take, or

treatment, any more than he subscribed to the early 19th-century "Bloody Code" which hanged children for stealing pork pies.

Dickens believed in capital punishment for extreme crimes – but hated public executions, or so-called "hang fairs" (abolished shortly after the publication of *Great Expectations*). Had Magwitch survived to be hanged at Tyburn thousands of Londoners would have watched in a

carnival atmosphere. That, as he recorded, had always disgusted Dickens. One can't help thinking it was at least partly the reason that he had Magwitch (unlike Fagin in *Oliver Twist*) die in the condemned cell before the hangman could do his grisly work, with a prayer for forgiveness on his lips, rather than struggling for his last lungful of air. Hanging should be, Dickens believed, a very solemn thing.

About the other

Miss Havisham's, which isn't destined for him. In the circumstances, the critics who condemn Pip's behaviour would probably have felt the same sense of horror.

Dickens's art has led up to this moment from the beginning. The secret bond between Pip and Magwitch is established in the early chapters, and Pip is always being reminded of Magwitch, and of what Robin Gilmour calls "the ambiguities surrounding his rise in station". Convicts constantly appear. When Pip first returns to his home town in chapter 28, for example, he travels on the coach with two, recognising one of them as the man who had given him two one-pound notes at The Three Jolly Bargemen in chapter 10.

"extreme punishment", transportation, Dickens had rather positive views. It was good for the empire, which was very much in its favour. Three of his own sons were packed off to the colonies to make their way in the world. Two of them died and were buried in the Queen's overseas realms. The last convicts had been transported to Australia a couple of years before *Great Expectations* was published. Looking back on the scheme, which had run for almost 150 years, Dickens did not think it had been an entirely bad way to deal with otherwise incorrigible criminals. The fact that Magwitch, a hopeless case in England, does so well as a sheep farmer in Australia reflects Dickens's conviction that emigration (voluntary or involuntary) was good for England, good for the empire and could, as with Magwitch, be good for the criminal.◆

Herbert, who has come to see him off, reacts with revulsion – "What a degraded and vile sight it is!" – and Pip can see why he thinks this:

> *The great numbers on their backs, as if they were street doors; their coarse mangy ungainly outer surface, as if they were lower animals; and the way in which all present looked at them and kept from them; made them (as Herbert had said) a most disagreeable and degraded spectacle. (28)*

Yet while to Herbert, the born gentleman, the convicts seem a different species, Pip has reason to know they are human and, says Gilmour, "in that secret part of his consciousness where so much of the action of *Great Expectations* takes place he can feel compassion for them", imagining the awful prison-ship which awaits them:

> *In my fancy, I saw the boat with its convict crew waiting for them at the slime-washed stairs, – and again heard the gruff "Give way, you!" like an order to dogs – and again saw the wicked Noah's Ark lying out on the black water. (28)*

On the road to Rochester the convicts begin discussing the pound note incident and Pip is filled with terror. Torn between sympathy for the men and fear that he will be recognised and discredited, he leaves the coach at the outskirts of town:

I could not have said what I was afraid of, for my fear was altogether undefined and vague, but there was a great fear upon me. As I walked on to the hotel, I felt that a dread, much exceeding the mere apprehension of a painful and disagreeable recognition, made me tremble. I am confident that it took no distinctness of shape, and that it was a revival for a few minutes of the terror of childhood. (28)

The irony here is masterly, with Dickens managing both to withhold the truth about Pip's expectations while simultaneously hinting at it, so that when Magwitch eventually shows his hand the knowledge – as in the climax of *Oedipus Rex*, when the hero discovers who his parents are – seems inevitable, something which has been there from the beginning in his behaviour and history.

Yet if it seems inevitable it is also startling, as if a man-trap has closed on Pip. Magwitch is the embodiment of everything he has tried to escape, a violent criminal who, for all Pip knows, may have blood on his hands. He has also, we shouldn't forget, turned Pip himself into a criminal, the theft of a pork pie and a file to enable a convict to escape prison being a flagrantly felon act – a capital crime, no less. At the period *Great Expectations* is set children scarcely older than Pip could be hanged for stealing loaves of bread. It was common in the 18th century and as late as

*Robert De Niro and Jeremy Kissner in a 1998 film
adaptation of the novel directed by Alfonso Cuarón*

TEN FACTS
ABOUT *GREAT EXPECTATIONS*

1.
Great Expectations, the 13th of Dickens's 15
completed full-length novels, was written in the
most tormented year of his life. He had broken up
from his wife, contracted venereal disease and
still not established a sound – adulterous –
relationship with the young actress, Ellen Ternan.
Biographers have speculated that Ternan's early
behaviour to him influenced his portrayal of the
cold, ungiving, tantalising Estella.

2.

Great Expectations is one of only two Dickens novels to be written in the first person – the other is *David Copperfield* (though he uses the autobiographical form in part of *Bleak House)*.

3.

There are, it is calculated, some 16,000 characters in Dickens's fiction and some 180 identifiable characters in *Great Expectations*. Oddly, we do not know the names, or full names, of two characters who play an important part in the plot: "Mrs Joe" and "Trabb's Boy".

4.

By the best reckoning we can make Pip is born in 1802 (some 10 years before Dickens) and his first encounter with Magwitch takes place in 1809. His second encounter – and the crisis in the action – takes place when he is 23: in 1825, or thereabouts. The novel begins during the Peninsular War. Pip is 13 when the Battle of Waterloo is won. He grows up during the Regency and the novel climaxes in the turbulent time before the great Reform Act of 1832. None of this history is alluded to in *Great Expectations*. Thackeray's *Vanity Fair*, which covers the same historical period (1812—28), is replete with socio-historical reference.

5.

The "hulks" – decommissioned navy vessels –
came into use after the American revolution,
which made transportation to that former colony
impossible. Australia then became a favourite
destination. Prior to their passage, convicts were
held in these makeshift and famously unhealthy
floating prisons, moored in the Thames and
Medway estuaries. The last hulk was burned at
Woolwich in 1857, shortly before *Great
Expectations* was written.

6.

In his notes for the novel (few of which survive)
Dickens worked out the ages of the principal
characters at the climax: Pip, Estella, and Herbert,
all 23; Magwitch, 60; Compeyson, 52; Miss
Havisham, 56; Biddy, 24; Joe, 45; Jaggers, 55;
Wemmick, 50. Mrs Joe, we may calculate, is some
20 years older than Pip.

7.

Pip is an inveterate reader, but we only know one
book he has read. In chapter 40 he says that the
reappearance of Magwitch in his life recalls "the
imaginary student pursued by the misshapen
creature". He has read *Frankenstein*, published in
1818, seven years before Magwitch's return.

8.

In chapter 44 Pip undertakes a midnight walk from Rochester to London, a distance of 26 miles. It was a feat Dickens, a fanatic walker, often did himself – typically at night. (He was a light sleeper who couldn't nod off at all unless his head was pointing due north. To make sure of this he always carried a compass with him; if necessary, beds were shifted.)

9.

One mystery of the novel is how Magwitch, the convict, manages to swim to shore from the Hulks with a "great iron" (a manacle) on his leg. The answer may be that Dickens (a good swimmer himself) intended to endow Magwitch with superhuman power.

10.

Dickens loved to include private jokes in his fiction. The unpleasant Bentley Drummle who marries Estella, for example, is named after a publisher whom Dickens believed had exploited and cheated him as a young author. He never forgot or forgave "the Brigand of Burlington Street", as he called Richard Bentley.

1831 a boy of 10 was publicly hanged for arson. The Artful Dodger in *Oliver Twist* is tried in an adult court, and transported (for stealing handkerchiefs). He is lucky to escape joining Fagin at the end a rope in front of a jeering crowd. And as Pip leaves the misty marsh to commit his first criminal act, he looks up and see "a gibbet

DICKENS AT WORK,
BY HIS ELDEST SON
CHARLEY

"No city clerk was ever more methodical or orderly than he.... At something before ten he would sit down – every day, with very rare exceptions – to his desk which, as to its papers, its writing material, and the quaint little bronze figures which he delighted in having before him, was as neat and orderly as everything else in and about the house, and would there remain until lunch time – sometimes, if he were much engrossed with any particular point or had something in hand which he was very anxious to finish there and then, until later. Whether he could get on satisfactorily with the work in hand mattered nothing. He had no faith in the waiting-for-inspiration theory, nor did he fall into the opposite error of forcing himself willy-nilly to turn out so much manuscript each day, as was Mr Anthony Trollope's plan, for instance. It was his business to sit at his desk during just those particular hours in the day, my father used to say, and, whether the day turned out well or ill, there he sat accordingly."◆

with some chains hanging in it which had once held a pirate". Suspended over Pip throughout the novel is Mrs Joe's grim prophecy that he is "born to be hanged", a fate made much more likely by his entanglement with Magwitch.

Nor does his criminal career stop in his seventh year with the absconded pork pie. Magwitch, by returning to London from Australia, where he has been sentenced to remain for the course "of his natural life", commits a second capital crime and it is Pip's bounden duty to report him to the authorities. "It is Death!" as he sombrely tells Pip – death dangling at the end of the hangman's rope he was earlier lucky to escape.

Instead of doing what an honest citizen should, Pip, once he learns the truth, makes himself an accomplice by giving Magwitch shelter, a false identity, and providing the means to escape English justice in Europe. On his way to Holland, Magwitch commits another capital crime, his third, and the one for which he is condemned to hang, when he murders Compeyson. Pip is criminally involved in all this.

In the real world, Pip would have been – at the very least – questioned by the authorities and, most likely, have faced court proceedings and quite likely have gone to prison, or have been himself transported, for helping Magwitch. Dickens decided not to complicate his novel by pursuing this, but Pip's criminality is real nonetheless, a dark fact which is powerfully there in his indelible sense of having done wrong.

The links between Pip and Magwitch are shown in subtle as well as obvious ways. There is a symmetry in that they have parallel childhoods, geographically: whereas Pip begins his life in Kent, Magwitch begins his in Essex, on the other side of the Thames. And just as the novel begins with Pip remembering the moment in the graveyard when he first recognised the "identity of things", so Magwitch has a similar moment of recognition about about his own childhood when he tells Pip his story:

> I've no more notion where I was born than you have – if so much. I first became aware of myself down in Essex, a thieving turnips for my living. (42)

The capital crime for which Magwitch is a convict when he first meets Pip is significant, too: he is charged with "putting stolen notes in circulation", along with Compeyson, whose business is "swindling, handwriting, forging stolen bank-note passing, and such-like". Steven Connor sees a pun here, with the crucial word "forge" re-establishing "the unconscious link between Pip and Magwitch and between legitimacy and criminality": Pip gives up his secure life in a forge because of his association with a forger; it is a link which is first made by Mrs Joe, who tells Pip: "People are put in the Hulks because they murder, and because they rob, and forge, and do all sorts of bad." The idea of forgery, and swindling, is important: it suggests Pip's alienation, says Connor: he gives up a world which is true for one which is false.

There is further irony in the fact that the man Pip first sees as a wild beast is in his way a nightmare version of the Victorian self-made man. Magwitch has set out to make money with a single-mindedness which makes his career in Australia a bizarre parody of an economic success story. " I lived rough," he tells Pip, echoing the paternal hopes of first-generation wealth, "that you should live smooth; I worked hard so you should be above work." (39)

And Magwitch, we finally discover, is not only Pip's benefactor but the father of Estella, the "proud and refined" girl whom Pip loves and sees as the very emblem of civilised life. Underneath she is not proud and refined at all, but shares her father's animal energy and passion. Indeed the "moral pattern" of *Great Expectations*, says Robin Gilmour,

> is only fulfilled when, in chapter 48, Jaggers hints that Bentley Drummle will beat Estella, and Pip, glancing at Molly's knitting fingers and flowing hair, realises that this woman is the mother of the

girl he loves. The wheel has come full circle; the girl who had been the inspiration for his attempt to improve himself is found in the end to be the daughter of a transported convict and a "wild beast tamed" (24), a woman so violent and powerful that she has been able to strangle another woman with her bare hands. And what in a lesser novelist would be a melodramatic linkage is here a symbolic structure of deep imaginative power and social implication.

Magwitch, then, is the source of all Pip's expectations, and when Pip recoils from him he is, in effect, recoiling from the unpleasant social origins of the money that makes gentility possible. By relating not only Pip but also the girl he loves to a convict Dickens points to the complicated origins of the Victorian preoccupation with gentlemanliness – not only how uncomfortably it was connected to a crude and violent criminal world, but also how it stemmed not just from a snobbish, class-based aspiration but from a genuine desire to escape a violent past and become a gentleman in the other sense of having a more decent and civilised life, of becoming a more "gentle" man.

Opposite: poster for the 1934 film adaptation of Great Expectations

How corrupt is the world Dickens shows us in *Great Expectations*?

The dating of *Great Expectations* is important. Pip, like Dickens himself, is born at the beginning of the 19th century into a world which was distinctly more brutal and unforgiving than the world of the 1860s when the novel was written: not only was life precarious – Pip and his sister are the only survivors of a family of nine – but the criminal code was cruel and primitive with its infamous hulks, squalid jails and readiness to hang children as young as ten years old.

Pip's first sight in London, significantly, is Newgate, where "an exceedingly dirty and partially drunk minister of justice" tells him that for half a crown he can witness a trial before the Lord Chief Justice:

As I declined the proposal on the plea of an appointment, he was so good as to take me into a yard and show me where the gallows was kept, and also where people were publicly whipped, and then he showed me the Debtor's Door, out of which culprits came to be hanged: heightening the interest of that dreadful portal by giving me to understand that "four on 'em" would come out at that door the day after tomorrow at eight in

the morning to be killed in a row. This was
horrible, and gave me a sickening idea of
London... (20)

Dickens clearly wanted his readers to feel
sickened, too, for the brutality of the criminal
code and the dehumanising way it is carried out
are stressed throughout the novel. When he died,
in 1870, as Philip Collins has pointed out, "the
system for dealing with criminals was recognisably
the one we have inherited; the system that
obtained in his boyhood belongs to another
world, at least as much akin to the 16th century
as to the 20th".

The system we are shown in *Great Expectations*
is corrupt as well as cruel. There had been earlier
novels with a Newgate background, among them
Daniel Defoe's masterpiece, *Moll Flanders* (1722),
and *Jonathan Wild* (1743), Henry Fielding's novel
about the great criminal hanged at Tyburn in 1725.
Jonathan Wild, like John Gay's *The Beggar's
Opera* (1728), was a satire directed principally at
Robert Walpole, the Prime Minister, seen as the
"real" criminal presiding over a rotten society.
Something of the same spirit is present in both
Dickens's earlier novel, *Bleak House*, and *Great
Expectations*, where the legal system, and those
who practise it, are seen as just as "guilty" as the
criminals they punish.

The London Pip arrives in is "ugly, crooked,

narrow and dirty", words which apply as much to its spirit as its physical characteristics, and Pip's description of "the great black dome of Saint Paul's bulging at me from behind a grim stone building which a bystander said was Newgate prison", leaves us in no doubt that this is a world in which prison matters more than church. Nor is it an accident that Dickens places Mr Jaggers's office in "Little Britain, just out of Smithfield", the lawyer's corrupt practice being an allegory for the official life of Britain itself.

Q.D. Leavis thinks – though her view is by no means generally accepted – that Jaggers may be "Dickens's greatest success in any novel". Pip's introduction to his office reveals that his abilities and labour are almost entirely devoted to the cause of *defeating* rather than serving the purpose of justice, for which he has earned not just wealth but a high reputation. When Pip sees Jaggers at work in a police court, "he seemed to be grinding the whole place like a mill", terrifying prisoners, witnesses and officials. With his characteristic gesture of chewing his forefinger, he lives for the exercise of power, bullying everyone around him – "he even seemed to bully his sandwich as he ate it," says Pip. (20) Jaggers is "the letter of the law" personified. If the law, under the provisions of the so-called "Bloody Code" (abolished in 1835), hangs children and petty thieves, so be it. That is the law. Jaggers is as much an instrument of it as

Jean Simmons as Miss Havisham in David Lean's 1946 adaptation

the sword in the hand of the blindfolded statue of Justice. Two "ghastly" death masks of men whom, as a prosecutor, he sent to the gallows, preside over his office. His housekeeper, Molly (Estella's mother), is bound to him, as a prisoner not a servant, by his having "got her off" from a charge of murder. One of the more horrible moments in the novel is the scene at the dinner party Jaggers gives for Pip, Herbert and Drummle in which he forces Molly to show her "disfigured" wrist (presumably the sign of an attempted suicide):

PIP'S RELIABILITY AS A NARRATOR

Pip, most will believe, is an honest chronicler of his life. But he shows his capacity for make-believe when he tells Mrs Joe about Satis House. So: is Miss Havisham's house really as Gothic as Pip describes (or Wemmick's "castle" as absurd)? Is Bentley Drummle – the "Spider" – really as unpleasant as Pip describes him, or is the description envenomed by the spurned lover's jealousy? Pip's perception of things is demonstrably flawed. A more thoughtful young man might not, for example, have leapt to the conclusion that Miss Havisham was his patroness. Dickens makes this point in the narrative by introducing the wildly improbable scene of Pip on the coach home hearing two convicts talking about a third convict who, ten years ago, wanted to give an unknown little boy

"If you talk of strength," said Mr Jaggers. "I'll show you a wrist. Molly, let them see your wrist. Her entrapped hand was on the table, but she had already put her other hand behind her waist. "Master," she said, in a low voice, with her eyes attentively and entreatingly fixed upon him. "Don't." (26)

Whether or not he sexually abuses Molly – the hint seems broad enough – it is clear from this episode that in this world of "beaters" and "cringers" Jaggers is a sadist. Yet even Jaggers

money for being kind to him. Pip, currently in receipt of his "expectations" and spending every penny of it, should surely have put two and two together (many readers fresh to the novel will pick up the hints clearly enough).

Dickens does nothing accidentally in his fiction. He can subvert Pip's reliability as a narrator by use of a single word. Take, for example, the most sentimental scene in the novel – the death of Magwitch, at the end of chapter 56. Pip, after telling the dying man about Estella, describes how his head "dropped quietly on his breast":

Mindful, then, of what we had read together, I thought of the two men who went up into the Temple to pray, and I knew there were no better words that I could say beside his bed, than "O Lord, be merciful to him a sinner!"

Dickens usually restrains himself from overt religious reference in his fiction. In his life he seems to have been dutiful in observance, but lukewarm in his devotion to his church. (He seems to feel guilty: he is constantly washing his hands as if to avoid being contaminated by the horrors he deals with in his everyday life. There is a deliberate echo here of Pontius Pilate. Moreover, the soap we are told is scented – a sinister detail. (Pip smells him before he sees him, when they first meet on the stairs at Satis House.) While he represents something hard and inhuman at the core of British society, he is clearly aware that he is operating in a perverted and unjust system which he feels powerless to change, even if he wished to.

loathed Catholicism and evangelicalism for their extremism.) But he knew his Bible. Indeed, in a typically grand Dickensian act he rewrote the New Testament for his ten children as "The Life of Our Lord". Those as familiar with the gospels as Dickens was will be struck forcibly by the gross misquotation, "O Lord, be merciful to him, a sinner!" As it reads in Luke 18:13 it should, of course, be 'to *me* a sinner'. Is the pharisaism here (thanking God that he is not as other men – specifically Magwitch – are)

deliberately inserted to subvert Pip? Or is it a wholly permissible rephrasing to fit an extraordinary moment? If he wanted to misquote, why did Dickens not write "us, we sinners"? It was not a slip of the pen. In the reading version of this scene, which he prepared for delivery years later, Dickens retained "him a sinner". The question mark over Pip quivers at such moments in the text. We must assume Dickens wanted it to be there and for it to shake our faith in Pip as always "reliable".◆

In a rare moment of confidence he explains to Pip how it might be that a lawyer like himself might get a child from a woman who can't confess to being the mother – because it will go against the evidence produced at her trial – and so give the child to Miss Havisham who wants to adopt a girl:

Put the case that he [the lawyer] lived in an atmosphere of evil, and that all he saw of children was, their being generated in great numbers for certain destruction. Put the case that he often saw children, solemnly tried at a criminal bar, where they were being held up to be seen; put the case that he habitually knew of their being imprisoned, whipped, transported, neglected, cast out, qualified in all ways for the hangman, and growing up to be hanged. Put the case that pretty nigh all the children he saw in his daily business life, he had reason to look upon as so much spawn, to develop into the fish that were to come into his net, to be prosecuted, defended, forsworn, made orphans, bedevilled somehow... (51)

If Jaggers behaves as he does because he is heartless, his assistant, Wemmick, exists as a kind of corrective: caught up in the same unpleasant world, Wemmick holds guilt at bay by keeping his office life and his private life entirely separate. His intrinsic goodness is expressed in a schizophrenia which amounts almost to a kind of madness, a madness as distinctive, in its way, as Miss Havisham's. It is this which enables him to survive. Like Jaggers, he has been party to having men, women and children hanged who did not deserve to die – and part of him is dehumanised to the extent that he seems no longer flesh and blood:

> *Casting my eyes on Mr Wemmick as we went along... I found him to be a dry man, rather short in stature, with a square wooden face, whose expression seemed to have been imperfectly chiselled out with a dull-edged chisel. (21)*

But when he makes his way home across the river, Wemmick becomes a human being again. Behind the drawbridge in the Castle on the Walworth Road, he is a loving son to an ailing father and helps Pip in a way he wouldn't dream of doing in his official capacity.

The sense of a society where justice is arbitrary and which butchers people as callously as animals – the novel makes a point of the proximity of Newgate to Smithfield – is maintained to the end. Compeyson is a vicious criminal, unlike Magwitch, but, because of his respectable background, treated much more leniently. When Magwitch (whose first name, Abel, reminds us of the biblical twin murdered by Cain) comes to trial, the Judge's comments bear no relation to any just interpretation of what has happened, the "official" version being very different from the version Pip knows. And when the judge passes sentence of death on the "two-and-thirty men and women" at once, we know that at least one of them has been made a criminal by the refusal of his society to do anything for him but drive him first to steal from hunger and from there to prison and a life of crime.

Is Orlick Pip's "double"?

Pip's realisation of the truth about his patron deepens his sense of guilt: it is for expectations based on Magwitch's money that he has deserted Joe. His guilt deepens still further when he returns to Satis House to learn of Estella's fate. His expectations, he now knows, have come to nothing; they have been built on illusions.

Feeling in his remorse more sympathetic towards Magwitch, he also comes to feel more sympathy for Miss Havisham – herself the victim of a heartbreaking deception. She, meanwhile, realises what she has done by using Estella to take revenge on Pip. In a scene which is as much symbolic as realistic, she burns up in what Q.D. Leavis calls "Dantean flames of penitence", with Pip kissing the dying woman's lips in forgiveness and his own hands and arms being scorched by his involvement with her. The underlying meaning of the scene is stressed further with Pip's reference to the dispersal, by the flames, of "the heap of rottenness and all the ugly things that sheltered there". (49)

The intensity of this episode prepares the way for the extraordinary scene which follows: another, equally melodramatic – and equally symbolic – encounter, this one between Pip and Orlick in the sluice-house on the marshes. Leavis thinks there are clear echoes here of *Pilgrim's Progress*, a book which was very popular in Dickens's time. In John Bunyan's story of a pilgrimage through the Valley of the Shadow of Death, the hero, Christian, has to meet and overcome Apollyon, the Devil's advocate. Once he has Christian at his mercy, Appollyon tells him to prepare to die and confronts him with charges of his guilt, just as Orlick does to Pip. Like Christian, too, Pip admits to his sins, hopes for forgiveness, faces death by flames and is wounded; and like Christian his assailant is only routed after he has given up hope.

Modern critics have paid a lot of attention to Orlick, their emphasis being less on *Pilgrim's Progress* than on the idea that Orlick in the novel is acting out Pip's suppressed desires, even behaving as Pip's "double" in a Jekyll and Hyde fashion. His career runs parallel to Pip's: he works for Joe at the forge, as Pip does; he assaults Mrs Joe but Pip is linked to the assault, too, and feels responsible, because he has supplied the weapon; he goes to

Satis House as a gatekeeper after Pip has begun visiting Miss Havisham; he lusts after Biddy, whom Pip seriously thinks about marrying; and he helps the unpleasant ex-convict (Compeyson) after Pip has begun to help Magwitch. In all these ways he appears to shadow Pip, and, in his own perverted way, seeks to better himself.

There are unconscious parallels, too. Orlick's hatred for Mrs Joe is, perhaps, the conscious expression of what Pip himself might feel towards his sister: she has beaten him often enough. And what Orlick does to Mr Pumblechook at the end of

"We sat down on a bench that was near," By F.A. Fraser c. 1877. The publishers Chapman and Hall called the reprint for which the etching was commissioned the Household Edition, *capitalising on fond memories of Dickens's 1850s' weekly journal* Household Words

the novel, when he breaks into his house, reflects an anger which Pip himself might reasonably feel towards a man whose patronising, bullying and unpleasantness he has cause to know all too well.

In his influential 1960 essay, "The Hero's Guilt: the Case of Great Expectations", the critic Julian Moynahan sees Orlick and his activities as standing for Pip's guilt, or, to use T.S. Eliot's term, as being the "objective correlative" for that guilt. Unlike Pip, Orlick is "unmotivated, his origins... shrouded in mystery, his violence... unqualified by regret", but the parallels between them are too strong to be anything other than deliberate.

Up to a point Orlick seems not only to dog Pip's footsteps, but also to present a parody of Pip's upward progress through the novel, as though he were in competitive pursuit of some obscene great expectations of his own.

Somehow Pip cannot keep Orlick out of his affairs. When Magwitch first appears in London, Orlick is crouching in the darkness on the landing below Pip's flat. And when Pip first tries to arrange Magwitch's escape down the Thames, his plans are thwarted by the trick which brings him down to the marshes to face Orlick in the hut. Moynahan writes:

Its lurid melodrama and the awkwardness of its integration with the surrounding narrative has made many readers dismiss this scene as a piece

A makeup artist touches up the faces of John Mills and David Jacobs during filming of David Lean's 1946 adaptation

of popular writing aimed at the less intelligent members of Dickens's audience. But the confrontation of Orlick and Pip on the marshes is crucial... because it is the scene in which Dickens comes closest to making explicit the analogy between the hero and the novel's principal villain and criminal.

The scene in the limekiln is like a nightmare, made worse for Pip because he feels some of the accusations Orlick makes are true: he *has* been socially ambitious, he *has*, in effect, repudiated early associates in his search for gentility and he is sensitive to the charge that he is the one really responsible for the murder of his sister:

> *... it warn't old Orlick as did it; it was you. You*
> *was favoured, and he was bullied and beat. Old*
> *Orlick bullied and beat, eh? Now you pays for it.*
> *You done it; now you pays for it.* (53)

Orlick here, says Moynahan, is presenting himself
as "a monstrous caricature of the tender-minded,
hero, insisting that they are two of a kind with the
same ends, pursued through similarly predatory
and criminal means".*

Peter Brooks, in another admired essay on
Great Expectations in 1980, also sees Orlick as a
"hateful and sadistic version of the hero" who
throughout the novel acts the role of Pip's "bad
double". The scene in the limekiln is appropriate,
in Brooks's view, because it is part of a pattern: Pip
is constantly returning from London to his home
town, and though the ostensible purpose of these
trips is to make reparations to Joe their effect,
every time, is to revive repressed memories of his
childhood. This is what happens when Pip
recognises one of the convicts on the coach on his
first visit home in chapter 28 and feels "for a few

*One question raised by Moynahan's essay is: was Dickens
conscious of what he was doing in his treatment of Orlick? Behind
the question lies a broader one. Dickens is widely regarded as one
of the great symbolists and his works are infused with poetic
imagery. But in his notes there is no indication he was conscious of
this. One must assume his genius was largely intuitive.

minutes" a revival of "the terror of childhood", and it happens on other occasions too. "Repetition as return," says Brooks,

> becomes a reproduction and re-enactment of infantile experience; not simply a recall of the primal moment, but a reliving of its pain and terror, suggesting the impossibility of escape from the originating scenarios of chidhood, the condemnation forever to replay them.

Whether or not we think of Orlick as Pip's "bad double", he plays a key role in the story in keeping the hero's memories alive. In the scene in the limekiln, having lured Pip back to the marshes, Orlick forces him to relive the pain and terror of his childhood in a particularly graphic and unpleasant way, part of Pip's terror being that if he dies prematurely, without explanation, he will be "misremembered after death... despised by unborn generations". The cycle doesn't even end once the threat has been lifted: when Pip afterwards tries to help Magwitch escape, the drama is played out in the Thames estuary, where "it was like my own marsh country, flat and monotonous, with a dim horizon". He is back once again in the muddy tidal flats of his childhood – a childhood he can't escape.

Is *Great Expectations* a misogynist novel?

Women don't come well out of *Great Expectations*. Mrs Joe, the first woman to occupy centre stage, is a sadist who curses, whips and batters her luckless brother. While we may not want to see her dead, we can be forgiven for wanting to see her get some of what she dishes out to the men in her family. And after Orlick has clubbed her into imbecility she does, in fact,

BIDDY

The critic John Kucich observes in *Repression in Victorian Fiction* that the frightening passions of Dickens's more villainous characters are somehow related to a lack of passion in his heroes and heroines. Biddy is not quite a heroine, but she is the strongest counterweight to the tormented women of *Great Expectations*.

Seen by some critics as irritating and too good to be true, she is the incarnation of gentleness and mild instruction; it is Biddy who, at the Dame's school, teaches Pip to read; she is – as her name indicates – "biddable". But she is also the soul of non-violence and goodness. It is she who cares for the brain-damaged Mrs Joe, making her in the process a forgiving, as well as a cringing woman. It is Biddy who "improves" Joe. It is Biddy who, without taking anything from anyone, makes herself a middle-class success in her little village world. And it is Biddy who, at the end of the novel – with a little "Pip" at her breast – is the image of motherhood in the novel.◆

mend her ways. "Her temper," we are told, "was much improved." (16) She even, at the point of death – as best as she can mumble – asks forgiveness for having been such a bad wife and guardian. But do women have to be beaten, or burned (like Miss Havisham) to "improve" their tempers? There seems, as feminist critics have often noted, something profoundly misogynistic in Dickens's handling of his female characters in *Great Expectations*. It is as if the novel endorses the ancient proverb:

> a woman, a horse and a walnut tree,
> the more they're whipped, the better they be.

In one way or another, the women who dominate the narrative are all witches: Mrs Joe, the sadist; Miss Havisham and Estella, both bent on sexual revenge; Molly the murderess. Miss Havisham even dies like a witch, by fire, though the fire first seems to improve her temper as being battered improves Mrs Joe's: in her dying moments, as we've seen, she asks Pip's forgiveness. Being beaten by Bentley Drummle seems to have the same effect on Estella. None of these women come to a good end; nor, the novel seems to imply, do they deserve to. It would, at the very least, be reasonable to infer from the presentation of Mrs Joe, Estella and Miss Havisham that Dickens had, at this period, a dark and savage view of women – and biographers have convincingly made the point that he did.

Lucy Frost, in her essay "Taming to Improve", argues it is only the women of "received Victorian ideas, pale allegories animated from without" who flourish in the landscape of *Great Expectations* – Herbert's pliable and faintly present Clara and Joe's Biddy. By "animated from without", Frost means they are not intensely realised as characters, unlike their more cruel counterparts. "They are neither interesting nor memorable, and yet it is into their company that Dickens tries to drive his strong females." The "strong females" have to be tamed to become more like Biddy and Clara, and they are tamed by violence.

In the early chapters, Mrs Joe is a frustrated woman imprisoned by her domestic role, a neurotic who has no scope for gratifying her desires and enlivens her life by taking out her frustrations on those around her. There is a sexual element in this, says Frost:

> ...one can scarcely avoid recognising how unlucky Mrs Joe has been in marrying a blacksmith who turns out to be the male counterpart of those Dickensian child-brides – sexless and dependable.

Yet suddenly, after her bashing by Orlick, she is

morally regenerated and converted into a placid goodness. Orlick gets her permamently off "the Ram-page" and gives her an entirely new personality. Can we really believe in the change? And why does she then become so bizarrely attached to her tormentor? Her behaviour is certainly not normal and, again, there is a degree of sexual perversity, says Lucy Frost, whether or not Dickens recognises it. In her new effort to be genial to Orlick, Mrs Joe, says Pip,

> *...showed every possible desire to conciliate him, and there was an air of humble conciliation in all she did, such as I have seen pervade the bearing of a child towards a hard master. (16)*

The simile suggests cruelty: while once Orlick taunted Mrs Joe – "You'd be everybody's master if you durst" – he now has the upper hand and she seems to revel in his mastery. When she wants to see him she draws the hammer which he habitually works with – "She had lost his name, and could only signify him by his hammer" – a tool that has phallic properties almost embarrassingly obvious to the modern reader, says Frost, even if they weren't to the pre-Freudian Dickens. The memory of Orlick's violence seems to please Mrs Joe, as if she has enjoyed being tamed through violence or at least, like Katherine in *The Taming of the Shrew,* accepts it as just. Much the same thing happens to Estella who – having once watched two men fighting with sexually-charged pleasure – is later tamed by a man who uses her, as Pip puts it, "with great cruelty".

Estella is more complicated than Mrs Joe. Self-protectively remote from affection, she is an illustration, says Frost, of Dickens's belief that childhood could warp someone's inner life to such an extent that sexuality and intelligence are severed from feelings. (Psychopathy, modern medicine calls it.) She is fatalistic, cynical and emotionally frigid, and Dickens insists on this frigidity, persistently showing that Pip is naïve in believing she is not impervious to love. Estella herself says that her coldness is her "nature... the nature formed within me". Well aware of her own peculiarity, she reminds Pip of it time after time. She may be cleverer than he is but she is not clever enough to repair the emotional damage of her own childhood.

"When you say you love me, I know what you mean, as a form of words; but nothing more. You address nothing in my breast. You touch nothing there." (44)

Estella's limited emotional range is demonstrated vividly in chapter 38, when Miss Havisham accuses her of being "an ingrate" with a "cold, cold heart" and she looks at her guardian "with perfect composure", saying, in a schoolroom analogy which underlines her coldness:

"When have you found me false to your teaching? When have you found me unmindful of your lessons?" (38)

She knows that her inability to love stems from being "brought up in that strange house from a mere baby", as she has put it earlier. She has been brought up, she tells Miss Havisham, starved of love – made, she says, to "turn against" the "daylight". How can she suddenly welcome daylight now? And yet, like Mrs Joe, she does. At the end of the novel Pip thinks the coldness has gone:

what I had never seen before, was the saddened softened light of the once proud eyes; what I had never felt before was the friendly touch of the once insensible hand. (59)

Powerless to help herself, Estella is freed from her frigidity by her brute of a husband, the character in the novel who is most like Orlick in his loutishness; like Mrs Joe she is tamed by violence.

Lucy Frost is unconvinced. How can brutality breed humanity? Is Dickens indulging in a fantasy which wipes out one kind of female character and replaces her with another? For while it is true that

Dickens's revised ending of the novel is, arguably, more sentimental than his original ending, both suggest that Estella has been chastened. The second ending is especially physical and brutal:

> *"I have been bent and broken, but – I hope – into a better shape." (59)*

This can only make sense, Frost thinks, if one assumes that Dickens wants to reassure the reader of humanity's "essential goodness": distorted personalities must be made whole; strong women must be tamed – good ones, like Clara and Biddy, giving proof of their goodness by doing nothing at all. They are there to help and sympathise. Minor characters like Mrs Pocket and Mrs Skiffens are merely cartoon figures who don't matter. In *Great Expectations* the women who do matter, the strong ones, including the hot-blooded murderess, Molly – the "wild beast tamed" – are all destructive, at least until men humble them. Frost writes:

One need not be a student of psychoanalysis to perceive within *Great Expectations* a deep-seated fear of women. The strong women are created vividly and are unquestionably memorable, but because their strength is negative and is associated with their ability to inflict pain on men, they must be "bent and broken" before they can win approval.

Of all the women in the novel, the most mutilated is Miss Havisham, and Frost finds her conversion as implausible as Mrs Joe's or Estella's, though she allows that the scene in which Pip holds her down during the fire is psychologically acute. Pip, says Frost, is here releasing his own destructive feelings towards her but doing so in an act which can be construed as morally affirmative, because life-saving:

> I still held her forcibly down with all my strength, like a prisoner who might escape; and I doubt if I even knew who she was, or why we had struggled, or that she had been in flames, or that the flames were out. (49)

Pip is master at last in this room where a vindictive wraith has so long held sway. But it is not just Pip's destructive feelings being vented in this scene, thinks Frost: it is Dickens's, too. To get free of Miss Havisham he has to give her a violent and painful death. The novelist himself seems to share his male characters' "vicious desire" to punish and break powerful women.

Perhaps. But to push this argument too far is to do less than justice to the subtlety of Dickens's art. Mrs Joe's "improvement" is *not* wholly implausible: her mind is disturbed by her battering; it's not inconceivable that she should change as a result and feel regret. Estella's softness at the end may not be entirely convincing but its significance can be overdone: as the feminist critic, Hilary Schor, has pointed out, the novel is written from Pip's point of view; we only see Estella through his eyes. And while she has been "bent and broken" by Drummle, as she admits, there is no evidence, except in Pip's imagination, that she has discovered a capacity for real warmth.

Nor does Miss Havisham's conversion bother all feminist critics. She is mad; everyone is inconsistent, mad people especially so; nothing in the narrative suggests she is incapable of regret, and her regret is only felt when she realises the terrible destruction she has caused. One line of

THE IMPORTANCE OF HANDS

Every Dickens novel has its master image. In *Our Mutual Friend* it is the river. In *Bleak House* it is the fog. In *Little Dorrit*, it is the prison. In *Great Expectations* it is the hand. We often know much more about the principals' hands in this novel than their faces. Who, when the name Magwitch is mentioned, does not think of those murderous "large brown veinous hands"? Jaggers? One's nose twitches – scented soap (the lawyer, like Pontius Pilate, is forever washing his hands). Miss Havisham? Withered claws.

Pip is brought up "by hand" –the fact is drummed into him ad nauseam by Mrs argument, indeed, sees her as reflecting a wider dilemma of Dickens's time. Elaine Showalter argues in *The Rise of the Victorian Madwoman*:

> The rise of the Victorian madwoman was one of history's self-fulfilling prophecies. In a society that not only perceived women as childlike, irrational, and sexually unstable but also rendered them legally powerless and economically marginal, it is not surprising that they should have formed the greater part of the residual categories of deviance from which doctors drew a lucrative practice and the asylums much of their population.

Joe and by Pumblechook – and his destiny, as "the blacksmith's boy" is to be a "manual", i.e. a "hand" worker not a brain worker (Victorians drew a strict division between the two).

After his experiences at Satis House Pip becomes pathologically ashamed of his "black hands". He wants to be a gentleman, he tells Biddy (whose hands are not, he notices, exceptionally clean). His great expectations include white gloves and a soft white epidermis inside them. Those expectations collapse and his hands are, literally, burned almost to the bone in the great Satis House fire.

Some recent critics have gone on to note powerfully erotic aspects to the hand imagery in *Great Expectations*. When Magwitch returns from Australia, to Pip's horror the first thing he does is slobberingly kiss Pip's gentlemanly hands – he, Magwitch, has, of course, made them kissable.◆

In their groundbreaking study, *The Madwoman in the Attic*, Sandra Gilbert and Susan Gubar see the representative woman of the time not as plucky Jane Eyre, but as Mr Rochester's mad wife, Bertha Mason, whose rebellion has turned on herself and who is imprisoned in an upstairs room in Mr Rochester's house. The madwoman is, in extreme form, Gilbert and Gubar suggest, the image of what society of the time did to women. Linda Raphael joins forces with them in seeing Miss Havisham's choice – if it can be called a choice – to live in the inner space of Satis House, "enduring the fetid atmosphere which threatens also to engulf young Estella", as repeating "the

PIP'S JOURNEY DOWN THE THAMES

In his *Life of Charles Dickens*, John Forster writes: "To make himself sure of the actual course of a boat in such circumstances, and what possible incidents the adventure might have, Dickens hired a steamer for the day from Blackwall to Southend. Eight or nine friends and three or four members of his family were on board, and he seemed to have no care, the whole of that summer day (22 May 1861), except to enjoy their enjoyment and entertain them with his own in shape of a thousand whims and fancies; but his sleepless observation was at work all the time, and nothing had escaped his keen vision on either side of the river..."◆

fate of many Victorian women". The images surrounding her – the remains of the aborted wedding – "visibly enact a gap between opportunity and desire" which frequently occurred in the lives of girls brought up to be "ladies". Spoilt in childhood by an over protective father, used to getting her own way, and with a limited understanding of the world, Miss Havisham is brought up unfitted for anything except marriage, and clearly susceptible to the smooth-talking, public-school educated Compeyson, who is aided in tricking her by her jealous half-brother. There were many who suffered like Miss Havisham, says Raphael, even if they didn't all go mad, and, like them, Miss Havisham doesn't really understand why she acts as she does and or why she is so bitter:

> We have no reason to suspect that Miss Havisham understands her own misery as a consequence of more than having been jilted. The tragedy of her life is not that Compeyson failed to show up at the altar; it is not even that he and her half-brother plotted against her – it is that she fails to understand the system that works against her.

Raphael, then, is one of several modern critics who applaud Dickens for showing things as they really were. It should be said, too, in his defence, that the principal male characters in *Great*

Expectations are as psychologically damaged as the women, and also meet unhappy ends. Nor does the book play down the effects of male violence – quite the opposite – or suggest that it can lead to any lasting "improvement": Mrs Joe and Miss Havisham both die and Estella, we know, will never be normal.

Dickens's view of women may have been a dark one when he wrote *Great Expectations* but so too, it seems, was his view of men. Miss Havisham's madness – concealed by a daily charade in which she appears sane – mirrors Wemmick's schizophrenia; her failed expectations anticipate and mirror Pip's. None of the principal female characters in the novel ends up happy, but then nor, with the exception of Joe, do any of the men.

How plausible is the ending of the novel?

Pip's rescue by Trabb's boy from Orlick's clutches is an important moment in the shedding of his illusions. Dickens delicately indicates this by having him wake up the next morning to find the mists have cleared: London appears bright and glittering in sunlight, "with church towers and spires shooting into the unusually clear air". It may be overstating it to say, as Q.D. Leavis does, that having faced death the night before, amidst feverish imaginings of being despised by Estella and her children, he can now be "reborn". But there is an element of symbolism here: he is subjected to tests by both fire (with Miss Havisham) and water (falling into the Thames with Magwitch) and is then finally ready to give up his worldly dreams and not only to accept Magwitch but to work for his benefactor's escape.

The journey down the river with Magwitch "freshened me with new hope", he says, though it is the hope of a life without great expectations. His sole aim is to help Magwitch and he holds the convict's hand, as he does later at the trial – a gesture which, as Dickens knew, would not have been allowed in a real Victorian court.

I saw a man who had meant to be my benefactor, and who had felt affectionately, gratefully, and

generously, towards me with great constancy
through a series of years. I only saw in him a
much better man than I had been to Joe. (54)

In what is a very schematic novel it is surely
appropriate that when Pip falls ill after Magwitch's
death, it is Joe who should nurse him back to
health in a scene which, as Robin Gilmour puts it,
"returns him, briefly and poignantly, to the old
physical intimacy and dependence of childhood".
But Pip can't be a child again, or recapture the old
companionship he enjoyed with Joe. There is no
going back.

Dickens makes this plain in a scene which has
often been criticised, Pip's return to the forge to
ask Biddy to marry him. He is shocked to discover
that not only is Biddy married – to Joe – but that
he counts for so little in her life that she hasn't
bothered to write and tell him this. The American
critic Ross H. Dabney argues that Pip finds "that
he has forfeited his right to her", and goes on to
argue that Biddy would have made Pip a suitable
wife. "Pip is now educated, but Biddy is a
schoolmistress," says Dabney. "In Dickens's terms
there is more of a class barrier between Joe and
Biddy than between Pip and Biddy."

This is simply not true. Village schoolmistresses
were not very well educated in those days, as other
19th-century novelists, like George Eliot, have
vividly shown, and the idea that Biddy would have

been a more suitable companion for Pip than for Joe is fantasy. Whatever American critics might think, says Q.D. Leavis, Dickens believed that "there are real distinctions to be made, based not on money or birth but on cultivation and intelligence and talent". Pip's aspirations to be a gentleman may have been based on illusions, and certainly don't bring him happiness, but the idea that he would be better off returning to the society of Gargerys, Wopsles, Trabbs, Pumblechooks, Hubbles and Orlicks is ridiculous.

Pip hasn't "foirfeited" his right to marry Biddy. She would be quite unsuitable for him, and he himself never suggests he believes she could make him happy: he offers to marry her to make amends, and to show how humble he has become. It is an offer made out of guilt, not out of love.

Dickens's decision to marry Biddy to Joe was surely the right one, as was his decision to change the ending of the novel, about which there has been much dispute. Originally, Estella was made to marry a new character, specially introduced for the purpose, after Drummle's death – the middle-aged doctor who tried to protect her from Drummle's brutality. She was then to bump into Pip accidentally in London, walking with Joe and Biddy's boy – and to kiss the boy, thinking him Pip's.

On the advice of a friend – the novelist Edward Bulwer-Lytton – Dickens changed this ending to one which seems both more realistic and, in a novel arranged so carefully, more in line with its pattern. That they meet at Satis House is no more of a coincidence than much of what happens in the novel; nor does it seem implausible that Drummle should have contrived to leave her a poor widow, with nothing but Satis House, though it is never explained how this came about. Like Pip, she has been humiliated and endured great misery, and they now have a common past which, as Leavis says, "fits them for each other and no one else". When Pip tells Magwitch, before he dies, that he has a daughter he also says that he loves her; his loyalty to his benefactor, if nothing else, would make him return to Estella and try to look after her. It is likely that Estella, for her part, would be less unhappy with Pip than with anyone else.

For any lobotomised Victorian reader this second ending might be construed as "happy", though if it is why is Pip's tone, narrating the story in middle age, so full of melancholy? When Pip says "We are friends", Estella replies less positively "And will continue friends apart". They leave "the ruined place", hand in hand, however, in a "broad expanse of tranquil light" – the scene is reminiscent of Adam and Eve at the end of *Paradise Lost* – and Pip ends by insisting: "I saw the shadow of no parting from her". Dickens agonised over this line. He had originally written "I saw the shadow of no parting from her but one", crossing out the "but one" at the last minute, deliberately to leave the ending more ambiguous.* The word "shadow" is interesting: Pip evokes it only to deny it but it hints that what Pip and Estella have been through leaves them with only a limited capacity for happiness. Yet the ambiguity of the ending suggests that while their expectations have been dashed, it is at least possible to *have* expectations, and difficult to live without them.

What view of life does *Great Expectations* leave us with?

The novel opens with two men attempting, vainly, to escape prison. At its end the same two men struggle as one tries to escape. He dies in a condemned prisoner's cell. In the same cell, Pip catches the fever which almost joins him in death with Magwitch. On recovery – narrowly escaping debtors' prison – he "transports" himself abroad for ten years, as Magwitch was transported by the courts.

Prisons dominate the world of *Great Expectations*. Satis House – locked, barred and

* The editions printed between 1862 and 1868 (during Dicken's lifetime) read slightly differently: "I saw no shadow of another parting from her."

chained – is as much a prison for its occupant as Newgate, the first building Pip sees in London. He has come to the city with great expectations and high hopes. "I felt that I was free," he jubilantly exclaims. He discovers, when the source of his expectations is revealed, that he is as much a prisoner as Magwitch was. Estella is a prisoner of Miss Havisham. As she tells Pip: "We have no choice, you and I, but to obey our instructions. We are not free to follow our own devices, you and I."

There are a series of references and allusions to *Hamlet* in *Great Expectations,* a play which suggests that Denmark is a prison and which is about, among other things, the way the past shapes the present. Pip dreams of playing Hamlet, though knowing only five words of the play, Miss Havisham's half-brother, Mr Arthur, fantasises about her as being all in white with white flowers in her hair, an unmistakable allusion to Ophelia, and, in one of the book's funniest scenes, Mr Wopsle gives a dreadful performance of the prince (chapter 31). Hamlet cannot free himself from what the ghost of his father wants him to do: Magwitch, rising up from behind the gravestones, has the same effect on Pip, and when Magwitch returns he, like the Ghost in *Hamlet*, comes in the dark, though heralded not by a "bell... beating" the hour but by the church clocks of London striking it. "I doubt if a ghost could have been more more terrible to me," Pip writes, when he realises who his visitor is.

As A.L. French says, *Great Expectations* is full of situations in which parents, or their substitutes, dominate and indeed determine their children – not merely what they do but who they are.

The novel is defining, long before modern psychology, the ways in which the child is father of the man; and there is a strong impulse in its art to see the man as being exclusively and solely the offspring of the child – to see the characters as altogether determined by their earlier lives.

Like *Hamlet* (in part at least), *Great Expectations* contains at its core an investigation of

Ethan Hawke and Robert De Niro as Finnegan Bell (Pip's character) and Prisoner in Alfonso Cuarón's 1998 film

psychological and moral determinism. There is a side to Dickens, says French, which wants to believe that people can grow and mature, and that suffering can be beneficial, and make the victims of it kinder, sweeter and more tolerant, but the overall message of the book, despite the novelist's conscious intent, is more downbeat, and more dismaying in its implications. It is more akin to Wemmick's description of Jaggers's methods: "suddenly – click – you're caught". Other modern, post-structuralist critics take a similar view. The novel is full of prisons, says Jeremy Tambling – even Wemmick's castle is a "prisonous" house – and full of victims. Pip may see himself, in his own mind, as an oppressor, but he is actually a victim and, while he may lose his illusions, he never really reaches any degree of "normality".

He remains something of the child – his name, a diminutive, establishes that; he is never in a position, he feels, of equality with anyone else; his dreams of the file, of Miss Havisham hanging from the beam, of playing Hamlet without knowing more than five words of the play, his nightmarish sense of phantasmagoric shapes perceived in the rushlight in the Hummums, and his sense of being a brick in a house-wall, or part of a machine "waiting to have the engine stopped, and my part in it hammered off" – all proclaim his "secret madness". His sense of criminality is fed by virtually each act and its consequences that he undertakes.

And though he says nothing about himself at the time of writing, there is no evidence in the book that Pip has changed since his experiences, or that his emotional state has developed. "You made your own snares, I never made them," says Miss Havisham, but it is manifestly untrue as she herself acknowledges when, before dying, she entreats Pip to take a pencil "and write under my name, I forgive her". Pip's snares have been made for him, by Mrs Joe, by Magwitch, by Miss Havisham, and the book suggests there is nothing he can do about it. Like the other main characters in the novel, he has been shaped by the world into which he was born. Indeed, says Tambling, *Great Expectations* "comes close to suggesting that in an understanding of society, the concept of the individual is unhelpful". Individual identity is a social construct, arising from the experiences the individual undergoes.

"Pip is forced to recognise that not only are the objects of his desire unattainable, but also that his desires are not really his own," says Steven Connor. Rather, he acts out the desires of other people, or their desires are acted out through him. "It is Magwitch's desire that Pip should become a gentleman, and Miss Havisham's desire that he should love and be abandoned by Estella." What *Great Expectations* gradually displays, argues Connor, is Pip's "alienation from himself". The revelations that Magwitch is his benefactor and that Miss Havisham only really wishes to break his heart both show "Pip's marginality in his own life". Pip himself says the same thing when he tells Miss Havisham, after learning the truth about his "expectations", that the events of his life are "not my secret, but another's".

But Magwitch and Miss Havisham aren't the originators of their own desires either: Magwitch's is the adoption of what Connor calls "a generalised social ambition" which makes no sense for him to fulfil in person; society has driven him to it as a form of revenge; Miss Havisham's desire comes from a wish to inflict on another the pain she herself has suffered. Like Jeremy Tambling, Connor sees the narrative of *Great Expectations* as showing how little freedom individuals really have to make their own lives and how much the characters are shaped by what happens to them.

Earlier critics, such as Dorothy Van Ghent, anticipate these post-structuralist arguments when they point out that Dickens's world is not a naturalistic one. The characters may seem relatively uncomplicated, taken separately – but *Great Expectations* suggests it is a mistake to see them as separate entities; people's lives are intertwined; each character seems to flow into others; personalities merge, one into another. Pip's childhood echoes Magwitch's; it is almost as if Magwitch becomes Pip's guilt in a concrete form – as if he comes to live *inside him.* In the marshes at the beginning, Magwitch threatens the trembling Pip with a "young man" who, he says, is hiding nearby:

> *"That young man has a secret way pecooliar to himself, of getting at a boy, and at his heart, and at his liver. It is in wain for a boy to attempt to hide himself from that young man. A boy may lock his door, may be warm in bed, may tuck himself up, may draw the clothes over his head, may think himself comfortable and safe, but that young man will softly creep and creep his way to him and tear him open." (1)*

The young man is not, of course, hidden "with" Magwitch, but "inside" him; it is Magwitch's imaginary, animalistic other self and it is as if this self then takes possession of Pip. The parent–child relationship is at the heart of *Great Expectations,* and while in one way Magwitch beomes Pip's "father", in another way, Dickens implies, Pip is Magwitch's father – in that he, Pip, as a member of society, must share responsibility, and guilt, for the way Magwitch has been treated.

This idea of "doubling", or "double characters" runs through the novel. Orlick, like Magwitch, seems to exist partly inside Pip; Dickens even has Pip call Orlick his "nameless shadow". A shadow can never be lost; it is as if the two men are somehow organically connected. Another example of doubling is Molly and Miss Havisham. Molly is Estella's mother, Miss Havisham her substitute mother; the former is a murderess – Herbert describes her as "a young woman, a jealous woman, and a revengeful woman, revengeful, Handel, to the last degree". The desire for revenge connects her strongly to Miss Havisham. Miss Havisham is also connected to Estella. "In the sense that one implies the other," writes Dorothy Van Ghent, "the glittering frosty girl Estella, and the decayed, and false old woman, Miss Havisham, are not two characters but a single one." *Great Expectations* is full of such parallels and doubling, and it is through this that

MODERN CRITICS

The Dickensian - a journal designed to promote scholarship on the author - was founded in 1905, though universities remained inhospitable to him for most of the first half of the 20th century. Then came the heroic first generation of Dickensian scholars – the likes of Humphry House, Kathleen Tillotson, John Butt, Philip Collins and Q.D. Leavis – who, between them, made Dickens a respectable subject for academic study.

More recently, in what is now a fully-fledged "Dickens Industry", his novels have proved fertile territory for modern schools of critical thought. New interpretations of *Great Expectations*, for example, owe much to it achieves its vision of human complexity. (In Wemmick we see the essence of the "doubling"; there are two of him throughout, one at home, the other at the office.)

The lack of naturalism is clear from the plot, which is full of staggering coincidences. These range from the improbability of Pip hearing two convicts discussing his "two pound notes" in a stagecoach ten years after they were handed over, to the battering of Mrs Joe by Orlick with a filed-off manacle. Why, with all the hammers and other utensils in the forge, would an assailant use that weapon? That Compeyson and Magwitch should have escaped the hulks just four miles from where Magwitch's daughter and Compeyson's jilted bride are residing is another improbability. *Great*

poststructuralism, which holds that literary works create their own meanings, and deconstructionism, which takes as its starting point that we have nothing to make sense of the universe with but language – and that language, particularly literary language, is treacherous. Steve Connor's astute comments on the meanings of "forge" in the novel reflect both these schools of thought: forge, he points

out, can mean two opposite things in *Great Expectations*: to make counterfeit things – coins or bank-notes, as Magwitch does – or "real" things, as Joe makes horseshoes in his forge.

Jeremy Tambling, in his belief that the novel calls into question the very notion of individual identity, also draws on post-structuralist and deconstructionist arguments – as well as on the views of the left-wing French

Expectations is, one deduces, a very small world indeed.

Other improbabilities are structural and part of the framework of the novel. At one level, it strains credulity to near breaking point that Magwitch should be the father of Estella who should, quite coincidentally, be the ward of Miss Havisham, who should, coincidentally, be the woman that Pip falls in love with. That Jaggers, a London criminal lawyer, should, again wholly coincidentally, be acting as solicitor for both Miss Havisham in Kent and for Magwitch in Australia compounds improbability to the point at which credulity is in danger of breaking down altogether.

But Dickens's fictional universe is not naturalistic, nor is his depiction of character. And

philosopher Michel Foucault. (Foucault's emphasis on the role of prisons in the modern world, and how important they are in shaping our thoughts, is very relevant to *Great Expectations*, argues Tambling.)

There are plenty of other contemporary theoretical approaches. The women's movement has fuelled new "feminist" interpretations, determined to "re-appropriate" canonical texts from male hegemony. Hilary Schor, Sandra Gilbert, Susan Gubar, and Linda Raphael all "decentre" *Great Expectations* from its traditional male heroes and villains (Pip, Magwitch, Drummle, etc.) to concentrate on Estella and/ or Miss Havisham – the oppressed female and the "madwoman in the attic". *Great Expectations* absorbs all these interpretations inexhaustibly – post-structuralist, if his technique in *Great Expectations* suggests how deterministic the world is, it also suggests, conversely, a vision of a world of loners. Indeed this is perhaps the defining quality of Dickens's world, as V.S. Pritchett once suggested. His characters don't so much talk to each other as soliloquise:

> The pressure of society has created fits of twitching in mind and speech, and fantasies in the soul... The solitariness of people is paralleled by the solitariness of things. Fog operates as a separate presence, houses quietly rot or boisterously prosper on their own... The people and the things of Dickens are all out of touch and out of hearing of each other.

deconstructionist, feminist, even post-colonial (the latter making much of Magwitch's years in Australia).

To take a final example, William A. Cohen's "queer theory" finds buried in the text – possibly, as with Freudian analysis, at an unconscious level on Dickens's part – a subtextual concern with sex, guilt, and homosexuality (e.g. in Pip's relationships with Herbert and Orlick).

Adventurously, Cohen reads the novel as a "masturbator's manual", with close attention to such moments as Pip stuffing his bread and butter into his trousers (intending to smuggle it later to his convict, Magwitch). "Like many avid masturbators," Cohen informs us, "Pip is deeply ashamed, and just short of growing hair on his palms, he transfers his generalized guilt on to his hands themselves."◆

Dickens's technique, says Dorothy Van Ghent, "is an index of a vision of life that sees human separateness as the ordinary condition, where speech is speech *to* nobody and where human encounter is mere collision". In so far as communication is possible, it depends on language and our grasp of it. *Great Expectations* is continually emphasising both the importance of words and how inadequate they are. In the very first scene Pip is trying to decipher the words of his family gravestones; later he tries to teach Joe how to read. Joe's efforts to communicate are highly solipsistic: his pleasure in reading derives from tracing the letters J and O in the books or newspapers he looks at.

From *Don Quixote* onwards, says Van Ghent, novels have drawn attention to the ambiguities of language and the difficulties of making ourselves understood. Absolute noncommunication is "an unthinkable madness" but real communication impossible. "Dickens's soliloquising characters, for all their funniness... suggest a world of isolated integers, terrifyingly alone and unrelated." The feminist critic Hilary Schor cites Pip's early effort to write a letter to Joe, an action for which, as Pip puts it, "there was no indispensable necessity...inasmuch as he sat beside me and we were alone". (7)

"That sense of 'alone' and 'beside' coexisting is key to the novel," says Schor. The solipsistic idea is reinforced, one might argue, by the emphasis on dreams: Pip is constantly dreaming – he even dreams of his expectations being cancelled and of having "to give my hand in marriage to Herbert's Clara". It is reinforced, too, by the atmosphere Dickens creates. The novel opens in mist, "towards evening" and closes, also in mist, at the same time of day. Much of what happens takes place either at night, or in half-light, when people can't see clearly what is in front of them.

Great Expectations is a masterpiece, probably *the* masterpiece, of what is called Dickens's dark period. Its picture of a society rooted in savagery offers few of the compensations to be found in the more comforting pages of *Oliver Twist* or *David Copperfield*. It is a society whose hallmarks are violence and isolation, where the idea of gentlemanliness, however laudable in principle, is one based on illusions; its vision is one of a world in which our actions are determined by our pasts, by the opportunities we've had, and by the language we've learnt. In the way it raises questions about individuality and determinism, it is a very modern novel, much admired by modernist critics and not surprisingly it continues to generate passionate debate and to retain its status as one of the most admired works of 19th-century fiction.

A SHORT CHRONOLOGY

1812 February 7 **Charles Dickens born at Southsea,** near Portsmouth, second child and eldest son of John Dickens, an £80-a-year clerk in the Navy Pay office, and his wife Elizabeth. He was one of eight children, only five of whom survived.

1815 Napoleon defeated at Waterloo.

1823 John Dickens, after being posted to London, is imprisoned for debt. Charles is sent to work in a boot-blacking factory off the Strand.

1827 Starts work as a solicitor's clerk in Gray's Inn, at a pound a week, but quickly begins to contribute to newspapers

1836 First book of stories, *Sketches by Boz*, vivid snapshots of London, published to great acclaim. Marries Catherine Hogarth, daughter of a music critic.

1837 *The Pickwick Papers*, his first major success

1838 *Oliver Twist*

1842 Visits America, which he dislikes, and in *Martin Chuzzlewit*.

1850 *David Copperfield*. Dickens begins editing *Household Words*

1856 Buys Gad's Hill Place, Kent, where he will write *Great Expectations*

1858 Separates from his wife and the mother of his ten children after meeting the young actress Ellen Ternan, with whom he has fallen in love. Begins gruelling national tour, doing public readings of his work.

1859 Launches All the Year Round as a successor to Household Words.

1861 *Great Expectations*

1867-8 Exhausting tour of America which nets him £19,000. By now he is afflicted with gout and his health is beginning to fade.

1870 June 9 Dies, while writing *The Mystery of Edwin Drood*. Buried in 'Poet's Corner', Westminster Abbey. He left £93,000 in his will.

BIBLIOGRAPHY

Books with Extended Discussion of *Great Expectations*

Brooks, Peter, *Reading for the Plot: Design and Intention in Narrative,* Knopf, 1984

Cohen, William A., *Sex Scandal: The Private Parts of Victorian Fiction,* Duke University Press, 1996

Collins, Philip, *Dickens and Crime*, Macmillan, 1962

Collins, Philip, *Dickens and Education*, Macmillan, 1963

Collins, Philip, *Dickens: The Critical Heritage,* Routledge, 1982

Gilbert, Sandra and Susan Gubar, *The Madwoman in the Attic: The Woman Writer and the Nineteenth-Century Literary Imagination,* Yale University Press, 1979

Gilmour, Robin, *The Idea of the Gentleman in the Victorian Novel,* Allen and Unwin, 1981

House, Humphry, *The Dickens World* , Oxford University Press, 1941

Leavis , F.R. and Leavis Q.D. , *Dickens the Novelist*, Chatto, 1970

Schor , Hilary M. , *Dickens and the Daughter of the House* Cambridge University Press, 1999

Van Ghent , Dorothy, *The English Novel: Form and Function*, Holt, Rinehart and Winston, 1953

Articles and Useful Websites

Connor Steven, "Forgeries: The Metallurgy of *Great Expectations*", *www.stevenconnor.com/forgeries/forgeries.pdf*

Fielding K.J., "The Critical Autonomy of *Great Expectations*" *Review of English Studies* (1961)

French A.L. , "Beating and Cringing in *Great Expectations*", *Essays in Criticism* (1974)

Gervais, David, "The Prose and Poetry of *Great Expectations*", *Dickens Studies Annual* (1954)

Moynahan, Julian, "The Hero's Guilt: The Case of *Great Expectations*", *Essays in Criticism* (1960)

Orwell, George, "Charles Dickens", *The Collected Essays, Journalism, and Letters*, Vol IV, eds Sonia Orwell and Ian Angus, Secker and Warburg, 1968

Perdue, David, The Charles Dickens Page, *charlesdickenspage.com/expectations.html*

Raphael, Linda, "A Re-Vision of Miss Havisham", *Studies in the Novel* (1989)

Tambling, Jeremy, "Prison-Bound: Dickens and Foucault", *Essays in Criticism* (1986)

The Victorian Web, *Great Expectations*, *www.victorianweb.org/authors/dickens/ge/geov.html*

INDEX

A

Ackroyd, Peter 28
Aged P 49
Arthur, Mrs 108
Atlantic Monthly 4
Australia
  Magwitch's return from 8, 71, 99
  underworld 19

B

Balzac, Honoré de 19
"Beating and Cringing" (essay) 24
Biddy 36, 90
Bildungsroman 12
Blackwoods 4
Bleak House 65
Bloody Code 60, 76
Brooks, Peter 88
Bulwer-Lytton, Edward
  ending changed 105
Bunyan, John
  Pilgrim's Progress, The 84

C

Character shaped by events 112
Chesterton, G.K. 12
Christmas Carol, A 4
Clara 92, 96
Cohen, William A.
Collins, Philip 75
Collins, Wilkie 4
Compeyson
  jilting Miss Havisham 8, 56, 101
Connor, Steven 70–1
Convicts 49, 61
Corruption 74
Crime 18, 25
  Balzac quote 19
Criminal
  Pip as 63, 68
Criminals
  Oliver Twist, in 14
Criminal Code, The 59, 74–5
Critical theory, modern 114
  feminist 90
  post-structuralist 110

Critics 4, 43

D

Dabney, Ross H. 58, 104
David Copperfield 65, 119
Debtors' prison 9, 11, 107
Defoe, Daniel
  Moll Flanders 75
Dickens, Charles
  biographers 45, 100
  blacking factory 11, 14
  class, and 32–3, 42
  dark period
  gentility, views on 10–9
  humour, use of 16–8
  orphans 16–7
  portrait *41*
  religion, and 79–80
  social commentator
  symbolist, seen as 88
  wife, leaving 14, 45
  working (description by son
    Charley) 68
Dickensian, The 113
Don Quixote (Miguel Cervantes) 118
doubling
  Molly and Miss Havisham 114
  Pip and Orlick 83, 113
  Wemmick (at home and at office)
    114
Drummle, Bentley
  description by Pip 78
  original in real life 67
  Orlick, similarity to 47
  "Spider" 78
  violent tendency 47

E

Eliot, George 104
  Adam Bede 29
  Mill on the Floss, The 12
  Silas Marner 29
Ending
  ambiguity 9, 107
  original version 96, 105
  plausibility 103–7

Estella
  animal nature 47
  coldness towards Pip 7
  disdain of Pip 44
  heartbreaker 7
  marriage to Drummle 47
  prisoner of Miss Havisham 107
  revenge on men 53
Expectations
  illusions, as 83
  truth about Pip's 63

F
Fielding, Henry
  Jonathan Wild 75
Film adaptations (stills) *5, 15, 35, 64, 73, 77*
Forge/forgery, wordplay on 70
Forster, John 12, 16
  Life of Charles Dickens 100
Foucault, Michel 116
Frankenstein (Mary Shelley) 66
French, A.L. 23, 49, 56, 109
Freud, Sigmund 22, 27
Frost, Lucy
  "Taming to Improve" (essay) 92

G
Gargery, Joe
  Biddy, marriage to 50
  gentle nature 36
  limitations of 37
  Pip, affection for 29
  treatment of
Gay, John
  Beggar's Opera, The 75
Gentility 14, 48
  Vanity Fair, in 10–1
Gentleman
  Compeyson, leniency towards 8
  Drummle, by birth
  Herbert as born 62
  Pip's aspirations to become 7, 10, 72, 105
  Victorian idea of 10, 13, 33
Gervais, David 43
Gilbert, Sandra and Susan Gubar
  Madwoman in the Attic, The 100

Gilmour, Robin 13, 28, 36, 47, 61–2
  Idea of the Gentleman in the Victorian Novel, The 13
Great Expectations
  beating as theme 24, 49
  Bildungsroman, as 12
  coincidence and improbability 8, 115
  critics 30
  doubling 83, 113–4
  education in 22–3
  ending103
  facts about 64–7
  film adaptations (stills) *5, 15, 35, 64, 73, 77*
  guilt as central theme 19
  irony 63
  key exchange 10
  literacy as leitmotif 22
  misogyny, accusations of 90
  "moral pattern" 71
  opening scenes 20
  prisons 107
  sadism 49, 79
  sex 42, 50–52, 92, 117
  "snob's progress", 30
  solitary hero 20
  summary of plot 6–9
  suspense 5
  TV adaptation 30
  view of life in 107–11
  violence 48, 50
Guilt 19, 78, 105

H
Hamlet (William Shakespeare) 108
Hand, upbringing by 28, 98
Hands, importance of 98–9
Hanging 25, 56, 60
Hardy, Thomas
  Jude the Obscure 30
Havisham, Miss
  bridal dress 6
  clocks stopped 57
  death in fire 8
  love, views on 53
  original in real life 44–5
  preserving Satis House 6

House, Humphry 41
The Dickens World 30
Household Words 44, *85*
Hubble, Mr 23
Hulks 6

I
Illustrations
Dickens, Charles 41
Victorian sketch from 85

J
Jaggers,
at work in court 76
bullying of Molly 78
Little Britain, office in 76
methods 110
opinion of Drummle 48
Pontius Pilate, echo of 80, 98
Jailfever 9
James, Henry 50
Joe, Mrs
attack by Orlick 7
name 36
prophecy about Pip 69
sadist 91
sexual frustration 92
violence against men 50

K
Kucich, John
Repression in Victorian Fiction 90

L
Language
Lawrence, D.H. 50
Leavis, F.R. 34
Leavis, Q.D. 19, 26, 32–4, 58, 76, 103, 105
Little Britain 76
Little Dorrit 98
Lucas, John 4

M
Madwoman in Victorian imagination 99
Magwitch, Abel

Australia 8, 71, 99
death 79
Estella's father 71
Hamlet's ghost, like 108
Pip's benefactor 8
Provis, alias 8
revenge on Compeyson 8
significance of 58–73
Marshes 6, 26, 89, 112
Misogyny, accusations of 90, 102
Mist in opening scene and ending 119
Molly
Estella's mother 78
murderess 91, 96
Moynahan, Julian 43, 86

N
naturalism, lack of 114
Newgate prison 4, 59, 79
background to other novels 75
Pip's first sight of London, as 107

O
Oedipus Rex (Sophocles) 63
Oliver Twist 14, 16, 32, 60, 68, 119
opening scene 20
Orlick, Dolge
attack on Mrs Joe 7, 91
Pip's shadow 83
Orphans 16–7
Orwell, George 38, 43
Our Mutual Friend 28, 98

P
Paradise Lost (John Milton)
reminiscence of 106
Parent–child relationship 49, 113
Pip
Biddy, asking to marry 104
childhood 89, 104, 112
Clara, dream of marrying 119
criminal behaviour 63, 68–9
"cringer" 49
Estella, relationship with 48–57
gentleman, aspirations to become 7, 10, 72, 105

guilt 22
hand, upbringing by 28, 98
Havisham, parallels with
    Miss 55
London 23, 75
Magwitch, bond with 61
narrative voice 24, 78
reliability as narrator 78–80
Orlick
    attack by 8
    shadow, as 83
snob 29
Pocket, Herbert
    Clara 92
    expectations, lack of 7
    fight with Pip 47
    gentleman, as born 62
Pocket, Matthew 23
Provis (Magwitch alias) 8
Prison
    debtors' 9, 11, 107
    Foucault's emphasis on 116
    Newgate 4, 59, 75, 79, 107
    Satis House as 107
Pritchett, V.S. 20, 117
Pumblechook, Mr 23, 37

Q
Queer theory 51–52
    Cohen, William A. 117

R
Raphael, Linda 101
Ray, Gordon 11
Ricks, Christopher 43, 58
Roscoe, W.C. 11

S
Satis House
    fire 50–51
    lure of 42
    Pip's first visit 55
    Pip's second visit 46, 56–7
    prison, as 107
Schor, Hilary 54, 98
Sex 42, 50–2, 92, 117
Shaw, George Bernard 4
Showalter, Elaine 99

Skiffins, Miss 17
Smiles, Samuel
    Self-Help 42
Snobbery 72
"Snob's progress" 30–41

T
Tambling, Jeremy 110
Taming of the Shrew, The (William
    Shakespeare) 93
Ternan, Ellen 14, 45, 64
Thackeray, William Makepeace
    Book of Snobs 34
    feuds with Dickens 33
    Pendennis 12
    Vanity Fair 11
Thames 26, 100
Tickler 28
Tomalin, Claire 45
Trabb's boy
    mocking Pip 31
    rescue of Pip 100
Transportation 59–61
Trollope, Anthony 33, 68
TV adaptation 30

U
Underworld
    Australia 19
    David Copperfield, in 17
    Oliver Twist, in 14
Universal guilt 19

V
Van Ghent, Dorothy 21
Victorian society, nature of 19
Violence 28, 50

W
Wemmick, Mr 7, 31, 81, 82, 102
Wilson, Angus 4
Witches 91
Women
    Dickens's view of 102
    taming of 93
    treatment of 91
Wopsle, Mr 28, 108

01273·204·999

MR
SIMON
WIGG

First published in 2012 by
Connell Guides
Spye Arch House
Spye Park
Lacock
Chippenham
Wiltshire SN15 2PR

10 9 8 7 6 5 4 3 2 1

Picture credits:
p.5 © Corbis
p.15 © Alamy
p.35 © Pictorial Press Ltd / Alamy
p.64 © Alamy
p.73 © Corbis
p.77© Rex
p.87 © Getty
p.109 © AF Archive / Alamy

A CIP catalogue record for this book is available from the British Library.
ISBN 978-1-907776-03-8

Assistant Editor: Katie Sanderson
Typesetting: Katrina ffiske
Design © Nathan Burton
Printed in Great Britain by Butler Tanner and Dennis

www.connellguides.com